GAME-CHANGING
STRATEGIES FOR RETAILERS

GAME-CHANGING STRATEGIES FOR RETAILERS

Written by

John Matthews

Gray Cat Enterprises, Inc.

ISBN 10: 1544026633
ISBN 13: 9781544026633

Library of Congress Control Number: 2017903319
CreateSpace Independent Publishing Platform
North Charleston, South Carolina

CONTENTS

Introduction

About the Author

John Matthews is the president and CEO of Gray Cat Enterprises and is responsible for the management of all consulting activities for the firm, which include retail consulting for multiunit operations, consumer marketing for companies launching products in the retail sector, and strategic project management for retailers of all sizes, large and small.

His thirty years' experience in retail management includes marketing and operations management; category management; mergers and acquisitions; facilities management; real estate and corporate communications in a spectrum of industries, including quick service restaurant, convenience store operations, and general retail.

In recent years, Matthews has performed consulting and senior project management for Quiznos, Sylvan Learning Centers, Starbucks, Global Partners, Potbelly Sandwiches, The Body Shop, Deluxe, Hungry Howie's Pizza, and Burt's Bees in both marketing and operations functions.

Matthews' views have appeared in well-known, respected newspapers and industry trade publications including *The New York Times*, *Convenience Store Decisions*, *Brandweek*, *Convenience Store News*, *The Chicago Tribune*, *The Chicago Sun-Times*, and others.

He has spoken before hundreds of business groups and appeared on numerous radio and television media outlets. In addition, Matthews has written two step-by-step manuals, *Local Store Marketing Manual for Retailers* and *Grand Opening Manual for Retailers.*

Prior to founding his own company in 2004, Matthews held senior management positions as president of Jimmy John's Gourmet Sandwiches and as vice president of marketing, merchandising, facilities, corporate communications, and real estate at Clark Retail Enterprises, Inc. Additionally, he worked for nine years in marketing management as the national marketing director of the Little Caesars Pizza Corporation.

Matthews was raised in Plymouth, Michigan, and holds a bachelor of arts in communications from Michigan State University.

Retail strategies in real-life terms

I have been fortunate. In my corporate career, I was a part of three very dynamic and growing companies, setting the stage for my personal growth. I was pressed into new areas of responsibility that stretched my learning curve in each of the businesses. It's not often that a head of marketing is also the head of operations and manages ancillary divisions such as real estate and facilities management. This wide and deep business background afforded me the opportunity to see retail in a full circle, as opposed to through the eyes of only one department. Connecting multiple departments stretched my business acumen further than I could have ever imagined. For that I am very grateful.

With *Game-Changing Strategies for Retailers*, I attempt to glean as much as possible of what I've learned at large companies as well as what I have learned from starting up my own company and distill it for the up-and-coming retail operator. This book also is for the experienced retailer who is open-minded and looking for a game-changing strategy to spark more revenue.

If you are looking for quick answers or the silver bullet, this book isn't for you. This book is about process and discipline to stay the course in both good and bad times. The intent is to help the retailer stay in business for more than a decade, not develop a fly-by-night concept that burns out quickly. Every retailer—large or small, new or established—wants that!

Read by chapter or cover-to-cover

For the small business owner or multiunit retailer, navigating through all the demands of running his or her business can be daunting. This book is designed to offer guidance in a myriad of areas that a small business owner or multiunit retailer will face. Although this book is not designed to be read cover to cover, it certainly can be. It can also serve as a resource for those looking to gain knowledge in a specific area of business—all in real-life terms.

CHAPTER 1

SMALL BUSINESS OVERVIEW

Overview

Running a small start-up business has its share of ups and downs. Since I launched my company in 2004, running my own small business has been both rewarding and challenging. It has enabled me to establish greater balance in my life, as I have reduced the administrative burden that corporate America places on its employees and replaced it with more time spent developing content for my clients.

Given the choice, running my own business is the best option for me at this stage of my life. I can work out of my house; see my kid on a regular basis; focus my work effort on content rather than administration; and yes, golf a tad. That being said, I am continually asked, "What is it like to be in business for yourself?" by those contemplating the leap from corporate to sole proprietorship.

While it is not for everyone, here are some of the points that you should mull over before making the jump to starting your own small business:

One-stop shop

One of the benefits of being a small business owner is the autonomy of "calling the shots". You are the boss and clearly can steer your company as you see fit. Many think they relish this set-up, but in reality, when it comes to being the self-motivator that is required to be successful—the go-to-guy—many fall short. Before you read any further, ask yourself if you are cut out to be the go-to-guy. If not, you can save yourself a lot of time and frustration. Simply stay in the corporate world.

Develop a business plan

So why is business planning so crucial? In a word, clarity. Investing time to develop a plan provides clarification of the company vision. In addition, it provides a mechanism to gauge the results of the business and the foundation for future growth plans. In the long haul, it enhances the company's value through fiscal responsibility, which provides the story of opportunity to any future investor or employee. Business planning is one part strategy and one part tactics, but where the sausage actually gets made is in the execution. Execution comes in the hard work necessary to carry out a plan and the accountability for your activities by tracking them. In the early part of this book, I will devote a lot of time to business planning.

Understand tax burdens

Regardless of the political rhetoric surrounding the tax code and its impact on small business, the fact of the matter is that a myriad of taxes are levied on these entities. I am shocked by how many budding entrepreneurs fail to understand the taxes that small businesses pay. My company essentially has one of the easiest business operating models that a small business can have. I invoice a few clients per month, receive a few checks a month, pay a few bills a month, and have very little inventory and/or depreciation of capital assets. Despite that, my tax returns are usually sixty-plus pages. Filing as an S-corporation, my outlay on taxes is between 25 and 39 percent in federal taxes, North Carolina state taxes between 6.0 and 7.5 percent, and Social Security and Medicare (as both employer and employee) of 15.3 percent, so nearly 50 percent of all my income goes to taxes and fees.

Replicate yourself

Given the fact that a small business owner is a one-stop shop, he or she needs to replicate him or herself wherever possible. Tools such as social media, telecommuting, and online collaboration have enabled small business owners to be in many places at one time. In order to be successful, small business owners need to tap these tools to maximize their exposure to potential clients and to reach customers outside their immediate area. Before these tools were available, my business was limited to Illinois, where my company was based. Since I have utilized these tools to replicate myself, I have had clients in fifteen different states.

Navigate third-party challenges

A small business owner wears many hats and relies on third-party entities for key alliances. When GoDaddy had its website and e-mail server outage in 2013, roughly 5.3 million small business websites and e-mails were knocked out. Small business owners rely on these support companies and, at times, are held captive when issues arise. While my company does not conduct a lot of commerce via my website, many small operators lost online revenue because of the outage.

Be wary of scams

Lastly, where there is a small business, there is a criminal waiting to prey on the unsuspecting owner. As an Illinois corporation operating in North Carolina, my company once received a letter from a group claiming to represent the state of Illinois saying that I needed to send in $125 for my annual minutes records form. Having been in business nearly nine years at the time, I was keenly aware of all my company's annual expenditures. I checked my previous years' payments and found that I had never paid this fee before. I then checked with my CPA who researched the letter and found that it was indeed fraudulent.

In short, starting and running a small business may be the best decision you ever make. Having the facts in advance is critical to ensuring that you are positioned for success. Once you fully vet your decision to start a small business, the rewards can be amazing.

CHAPTER 2

BUSINESS PLANNING

Time for Business Planning

Here it is, the master plan. This is by far the most overlooked item to be completed by entrepreneurs—the business plan. How someone can start a business without a plan is beyond me, but many do. Many fail as well. So it is essential to create a roadmap for success, and that is your business plan.

Business planning usually takes place in the fall with a focus on the upcoming year at a minimum. It's the time to gather all your business colleagues in a room to hash out the key initiatives for the next twelve months. The time to throw everything up on the wall and try to get *everything* done in the first quarter! "This is the year that all goals will be achieved!" is the battle cry. Every vision, idea, and strategy gets bantered about; shouts of "There are no bad ideas!" fill the air. The room is electric with visionaries exchanging ideas on how their idea solves all issues, yet year after year, it seems that plans never actually come to fruition.

Why is that? The intent was there; the energy was present; and ideas were flowing. That's the easy part—coming up with the ideas. The success of your planning doesn't rest on the ideas; it rests on *implementing* those ideas. Companies should foster innovation in their business planning, but more importantly, they need to create a business environment that enables team members to execute these ideas with an on-time, on-budget mind-set. That is where the work begins.

I have been putting together business plans for more than thirty years, and it is clear to me that the strength of a business plan's core rests solely on how well it can be executed. Each year I approach business planning as an opportunity, rather than a burden. I would rather invest the time up front to map out the upcoming year than leave it to chance to dictate my strategy. As this forces me to think strategically as well as tactically, preparing a detailed business plan in advance enables me to identify potential challenges in advance of actually facing them.

In short, planning allows the company to articulate a common vision to align resources and make efficient use of investment dollars. A company that is perceived to be a well-oiled machine is attractive both externally with investors and internally with employees through job satisfaction and increased tenure.

Strategic planning and goals
The first step is to identify the key company goals, which will provide the overarching direction of the plan. These goals should be focused on three areas: financial, growth initiatives, and alignment to the company's vision/mission. This provides the overall direction of the company by establishing high-level goals that will be achieved by tactical initiatives. The overall plan should cover one to three years, with measurement mileposts monthly, quarterly, and annually. While the plan is put in place at the beginning of the year, it should be revised throughout the year, based on actual results.

Develop planning modules
Compartmentalizing your plan by developing planning modules or chunks allows you to attack the plan in parts yet still maintain a cohesive vision. I have found that developing an annual plan made up of quarterly targets—a rolling quarterly forecast financial model—allows for a

cohesive structure along with the nimbleness to react to market conditions. At the end of each quarter, a true-up process to align results to annual targets needs to be completed and adjustments made, if necessary.

Develop noncapital initiatives

Each project initiative should have a corresponding project plan that monitors whether it will be completed on time and on budget. The detailed project plan should accomplish the following: a) identify all the steps to be completed; b) establish a realistic timeline for each step; c) identify and allocate the necessary resources for accomplishing the initiative; d) ensure that the initiative has been vetted for departmental interdependencies and potential conflicts; and e) ensure that the initiative is in alignment with the overall strategic plan.

Create a capital plan

Next, develop a capital plan identifying the amounts to be spent on the business to increase its overall value. While not all capital dollars are entirely discretionary—i.e., dollars invested for anticipated return based on growth—it is necessary to determine how capital dollars will be allocated whether for discretionary purposes or general maintenance. Projects that require capital are critical for company growth and must be managed to their desired return, avoiding shortfalls in return on investment (ROI) or issues involving capital creep. If you haven't done so already, setting up a capital committee to review expenditures before starting the project provides some assurance that it has been vetted against return on investment. Lastly, developing a post-audit process enables the team to review and monitor the progress of ongoing investments.

Business plan analytics through key performance indicators (KPIs)

Identifying key performance indicators for your business to use as benchmarks throughout the year is perhaps the most critical step you can make with regard to business analytics. Not only will KPIs help identify key shortfalls in the plan, but they will also narrow your focus in addressing the shortfalls. For instance, merely recognizing that you have a labor issue isn't enough when you consider the following possibilities: a) labor rates may be too high; b) overtime has exceeded its budget; c) the issue is regionally based, not across the board; d) man-hours may have exceeded their allocated budget, and so on. A myriad of triggers could have caused labor to exceed its budget, and KPIs enable you to drill down to the cause. KPI management requires a disciplined monthly review process that fosters a blended analysis that compares actual results to both budgets and forecasts throughout the year.

Fundamentals, cycles, and trends (FC&Ts)
Your plan, if done thoroughly and in advance, should provide an excellent foundation from which to work. But even the best plan has to react to outside forces that will influence your best intentions. Identifying certain fundamentals, cycles, and trends that may affect your company is a prudent way to develop a contingency plan in the event an outside force rears its head. A series of key FC&Ts should be monitored throughout the year. Certain FC&Ts may include wholesale pricing, weather, commodity markets, or labor market impacts that are out of your control. In my opinion, developing contingency plans for these outside forces at least gives you a fighting chance to react favorably.

Strategic review of plans/goals at year end
At the end of the year, do a thorough review of the plan and its process and discuss it with the team in order to make the next planning cycle more effective and efficient. Take a look at all the successful initiatives and the ones that fell short in order to identify where in the process the broken pipes occurred. Remember not to double-dip on the capital project's EBITDA contribution for the upcoming year—your budgetary baselines should move in concert with these investments. All projects that straddle the budgetary year should be rolled over into the new plan.

Business planning is the road map that identifies where you are headed in advance. As importantly, it also identifies roadblocks—in advance.

Your business plan should provide a common vision supported by tactical initiatives that ultimately creates greater value for your company. It may seem daunting, but by knowing your vision and its corresponding financial targets, you will have a better chance at getting there and avoiding traps in advance.

Executing Your Business Plan

Recently, I had a terrific session on business planning with one of my clients. I had written articles on the importance of business planning, but this session resonated with me. What was reinforced to me during our meeting was that, no matter how you approach business planning, ultimately you have to execute the plan through hard work. Much like when you hire a fitness trainer to help you work out, eventually you have to do your sit-ups. There are no alternatives.

The key here is execution. Many companies can develop a business plan but where most fail is in the implementation. Aligning tactical execution to the strategic overlays is by far the most difficult portion of the business planning cycle. Not actually executing the work is like working out by going to the doughnut store—you won't see the results.

Execution of the plan can be tedious, tracking results even more so. When you take shortcuts, the plan falls well short of expectations. It is not easy doing sit-ups, and there are no shortcuts to achieving your business goals. Focus on and accountability for execution trumps all other parts of the business planning process. Here are some points to consider:

Where do you want to go?

Set the high-level goals for what you want to achieve by year-end. This is the easy part, because most planners pick a growth target arbitrarily. "I want to grow 10 percent in sales" or "I want to improve my profits by 20 percent" are typical claims for a budget. This type of growth target is called a top-down approach, in which a target is selected first and initiatives to achieve that target are developed second.

How will you get there?

Another way is to build toward your goal from the bottom up. This means developing all your initiatives for the year and having them roll up into a top-line goal. This bottom-up strategy enables you to compartmentalize your plans in chunks, each identified to add cumulatively to the overall goal.

Do your initiatives achieve your overall goal?

Whether identifying initiatives through top-down or bottom-up processing, for each initiative, you need to develop a project plan with step-by-step tasks in order to determine how to accomplish it. Without this level of detail, the plan essentially grinds to a halt. This is the most tedious aspect of your business plan, but in my opinion, it's where the rubber meets the road.

Time line the initiatives

Once the initiatives are vetted for viability, they need to be time lined. This will help ensure that projects will not be competing against one another for resources. In addition, with a time line for each initiative, you can accurately account for contributing revenues as roll-ups to your overall financial goal.

Create measurement and feedback mechanisms

Much like the trainer in the gym ensuring that you do your required exercises, a measurement process—either internal or third party—will hold you accountable for achieving your plan. It never hurts to be accountable to someone, and reporting your activities forces you to execute according to your plan. Peer pressure is one of the strongest motivators.

Do your sit-ups

It comes down to this: if you want a flatter stomach, you'd better be prepared to do your sit-ups. A plan is what it is—a plan. It only works if it is put into motion and the execution of the plan is flawless. Failing to execute and to hold yourself accountable will result in missing your desired goals. There are no silver bullets in business—hard, smart work trumps all. In the words of Vince Lombardi, "The difference between a successful person and others is not a lack of strength, not a lack of knowledge, but rather a lack of will."

The Value of an Outside Board

Sometimes another set of eyes can make all the difference.

Small businesses are phenomenal entities, often started in a garage or at a kitchen table. The sheer energy of the small business entrepreneur wills his or her company to success. Hard work, long hours, and steep odds are the norm for the small business owner. Over time, the entrepreneur goes to the well daily to keep his or her vision and dream alive. It is often my way or the highway with the owner, but when does this potentially myopic approach run its course? Would it be advantageous for the owner to have another set of eyes look at his or her strategic plan?

At that moment, the small business may want to consider a board of directors: an elected group of people who oversee and advise a business and its operation—in a sense, another set of eyes. In most small businesses, the value of an outside board comes from combining the working knowledge of the entrepreneur with the advisory knowledge of key board members. This combination can enhance the growth of the company and provide alternative perspectives on tackling any issues at hand.

I have had the privilege of serving on the boards of four for-profit companies in my career and relished the experience. Board members contribute their vast array of business knowledge to a company that may not have been exposed to different business practices. That being said, here are some key attributes of a board and its directors:

Board of directors' duties

Boards represent the interests of the company and the shareholders, not members of the board. Directors are selected and retained to make certain that effective management is in place and to provide ongoing monitoring of overall management performance. While the board generally does not get directly involved in operational or personnel decisions in a broad sense, it does select and evaluate the effectiveness of the CEO and his or her potential successors.

Private company boards

Most boards are made up principally of independent outside directors who each has expertise in one or all the critical functions of the company. Board members are expected to become knowledgeable about the company and its operation. Directors typically are knowledgeable about the markets and channels served by the company and have time to invest in the success of the organization. In some cases, key board members may have core competencies that are lacking in the organization, e.g., project management. In addition, a small business should seek board members who have strong business networks as well as strong analytical and financial skills.

Finding independent outside directors

So where does an entrepreneur find his or her board of directors? I would find my board members through networking, predominantly through my LinkedIn connections. Other methods would be to seek the recommendations from bankers, lawyers, accountants, community leaders and friends. A small business owner may also look for recommendations from other company directors, professional director search firms or from the internal executive management team. No matter where the pool of potential board members comes from, the key is to seek directors that have similar business experience and product knowledge.

Education of directors

Once the directors have been elected to the board, it is imperative to bring them all up to speed on the company. A presentation to the board should include a thorough history of the company—both its products and its operating philosophies. Next, the company should communicate the geographic markets it serves and the vertical channels it targets. An overview of the company's financials should include a five-year look back and a forward-projecting operating pro forma (at least three years). Lastly, the current fiscal calendar budget and strategic plan should be discussed.

The role of the board

A board's job is governance, not operations. Running the company is the job of the CEO; in a private company, the board's role is more advisory than oversight. However, a prudent board does not rubber stamp the CEO's decisions, but rather holds the CEO responsible for the company's performance. The focus of the board is largely determined by the goals of the shareholders. For example, if the corporation is underperforming, the primary focus should probably be on the bottom line. If shareholders want strong growth for value generation, the primary focus should be on the top line.

Board member activities

Strategic planning is the most significant activity of the board. Many of the board members will have well-established business networks that can lead to new account and market business development. Board members can introduce the company to new prospects or help create opportunities for potential acquisitions. The board is the perfect entity with which to "war game" strategic plans, helping further define them through a review process. Based on its members' experience, the board may mentor the executive team, helping align its vision with concrete strategic and tactical plans. From a financial perspective, board members become the dart throwers in discussing the company's overall financial performance. This post-analysis review of the company's financial performance and the overall capital investment initiatives allow the board to evaluate financial performance critically and without bias.

Creating a board is an important step for any business, but it may not be for everyone. Most entrepreneurs are entrepreneurs because they like having control. Reporting to a board diminishes that control, but the tradeoff is that the entrepreneur may have a stronger organization in the long run.

General and Administrative (G&A) Budgeting

The next part of your business planning involves the general and administrative (G&A) budgeting section of your plan. This is where heads are counted, budgets are sandbagged, and perks are justified. It is an annual ritual that becomes a core tenet in the overall business planning cycle. Yet whether they are the heads of large departments or sole proprietors, most consider managing G&A expenses a necessary evil.

First of all, what is this thing called G&A anyway? Roughly speaking, these are budgeted dollars outside the direct expense associated with the creation of products or services. For example, unlike labor dollars to run a store—direct labor—G&A labor dollars are associated with the office personnel. While the operations group is held to a tight P&L at the store level, often the out-of-store G&A budgets are not held to the same daily scrutiny. In some cases, profits garnered at the store become eroded at the company level by mismanagement of these G&A budgets.

So it is time to take a close look at G&A as one way of managing to your desired bottom line. While I am sure these budgets were tightened considerably during the economic downtown that began in 2008, they still may contain fluff in their line items. Take a look at the top seven areas of a G&A budget, and ask the following questions:

Out-of-store labor

- When was the last time the organization right sized its support staff to add value to the field operations?
- Is there an opportunity to capitalize some of the labor associated with the company investments?
- Have the bonuses and performance merits been in sync with operational profitability?

Benefits and insurance

- How frequently are the costs of 401(k)s, workman's compensation, and other insurance reviewed?
- Is money invested for personnel welfare, tuition reimbursement, and employee education getting a bang for the buck?
- Is there wiggle room to reduce or combine offsite management meetings by 10 percent? By 20 percent?

Travel and entertainment

- Are company personnel held to a strict travel and entertainment policy?
- How much can you save by negotiating a standard rate at a hotel chain or rental car company?
- If out-of-store employees had to spend their own money on travel, do you believe that they would schedule their trips more economically?

Office occupancy

- If reducing paper costs is a goal, how close to being paperless do you believe the company could get, and how much would that save?

- How closely have you monitored utility costs and contracts including electric, gas, trash, telephone, data, and the like to squeeze savings?
- Is the current office right sized for the operation, or could the company make do with less space?

Professional fees

- What are the costs and benefits of outsourcing professional services as opposed to bringing them in house?
- What special projects can be commissioned that realize savings on a percentage fee basis?
- What internal preparation can be completed in advance of calling in a bookkeeper, accountant, or attorney in order to save on their fees?

Computer/IT-related expenses

- What is the company philosophy on technology—functionality or chase the next shiny object?
- Can technology advance to offset head-count increases?
- How does the technology strategy derive savings from the interface with the field operations?

Other expenses

- Has the company shopped around for the best bank fee structure?
- What parameters have been set with regard to memberships?
- What other expense line items can be renegotiated?

I have always been a tremendous believer in bottom-up expense budgeting, meaning that every year, the budget is not a carryover but rather a complete rewrite asking these types of questions. Over time, and unlike the government's baseline budgets with automatic increases, your G&A budgets will be tight. Employ this discipline in your organization and improve your P&L without a lot of angst.

Creating a Policy and Procedures Manual

As a small business owner, you may wonder why you would need to get organized from a policy and procedure standpoint. A lack of structure on how employees should conduct themselves at work, though, creates the possibility of inequality as well as abuse by employees.

Policy and procedure handbooks are designed to serve as guidelines for management and to create a set of rules that will be applied fairly to all employees. They are not intended to create binding agreements between the company and any employee or contractor. Rather, they serve as guiding principles for how the company operates philosophically.

The policy and procedure handbook helps set the stage for both existing and new employees. That being said, the company should reserve the right, at any time and in its sole discretion, to change, modify, delete, or deviate from any guideline in the handbook without notice. Remove the ambiguity by aligning the policies and procedures of the company and articulating them in an organized handbook.

Here are some of the items to address when developing a policy and procedure handbook:

Set your team at ease

The goal of the handbook is to set the bar for how employees should act within and on behalf of the company. The handbook should include a detailed code of conduct policy for employees. It should address training on harassment—both physical and sexual. In at-will states, explain that the employer is free to discharge individuals without cause and that the employee is free to quit, strike, or otherwise cease work.

Align expectations
The handbook should address standards for employees. Details should include guidelines for the use of e-mail, the telephone, social media, and other forms of communication. The handbook should outline the dress code for the company and establish guidelines for the office and field. In addition, all travel policies should be clearly outlined.

Communicate nonnegotiables
The handbook should communicate any information required by law, including the fact that the company is an equal opportunity employer. In addition, the details of the Family and Medical Leave Act (FMLA) and the Americans with Disabilities Act (ADA) should be included. The handbook should also include the workplace drug policy.

Manage time
Setting expectations regarding business hours in advance will help prevent time creep—employees showing up late and leaving early. Outline the holiday schedule as well as policies on vacations, sick time, and other days off. Guidelines for requesting a leave of absence should also be spelled out.

Help employees
Employees want to feel appreciated. The handbook should include a section on how new opportunities within the company are communicated as well as how employees can apply for these new jobs. Steps taken to protect employees from injury and other safety issues should be addressed.

Articulate the carrot
Outlining the company benefits program not only helps existing employees understand their coverage, but also details an attractive perk for prospective employees. If you align your team with a common goal for

company performance, the handbook can explain the compensation structure, including raises and bonuses. Make the handbook clear and concise and use it as an incentive for employees.

Keep it confidential

Lastly, every employee (and employer) should be confident that his or her personal information remains private. Guidelines on how reference checks are conducted as well as the management of employee personnel files should be outlined. Maintaining and preserving the integrity of the employees as well as the organization is critical.

Creating and maintaining a policy and procedures handbook helps both the employer and the employee understand the playing field at the company. Most issues arise because policies are vague. Taking the time to inform employees of expectations is part of the path to greater prosperity.

GrayCat
Enterprises, Inc.

CHAPTER 3

OPERATIONS

Store Design for the Retail Environment

One of the most important and biggest challenges facing a retailer is creating a new vision for a chain of stores, while simultaneously running the day-to-day business. There are only so many resources to go around, and carving out the time to not only manage the process, but also to create a new store vision is daunting.

With that in mind, here are some key items to consider:

It's not just about store design—it's about creating an experience

Experiences create emotional connections with your customers in order to keep them coming back. You need to start with the mind-set that you are creating a branded experience, which is much more than picking materials and finishes and trying to figure out store adjacencies.

Understand your industry

This is the first vital step to creating a long-term vision. It is important not only to know where your industry has been, but also to grasp where it's headed. All too often, retailers fail to embrace changes in their industries. Another valuable part of this step is to look at related best-in-class retailers outside your industry to see what makes them so successful.

Talk to your customers

Your customers are harbingers of things to come—watch and listen closely. The customers of your stores are not *exclusively* yours—they are your competitors' as well, and they visit other retail outlets that influence their perspectives. Gaining a better understanding of your customer prior to heading into your strategic process gives you a leg up on where to head.

This is an exercise of process and art

Managing the creation of your store of the future is a necessary part of keeping the planning on time and on budget. Whether you manage this in house or outsource it to industry experts, managing both the decision-making and the strategic direction of the design will make the difference in creating a cost-effective vision. It is good to start with a baseline budget and clearly articulate that at the outset in order to manage expectations.

Manage the process

Managing the process is critical to the overall brand design. Timely decision-making that is targeted and focused on a common endgame keeps your strategic direction and branding on plan. So how should you approach process management?

- Start at the baseline
  - Store audits. Visit existing sites as well as competitive locations both in and out of the industry to gain a baseline understanding of the business. Understand the good, the bad, and the ugly. Find the voids in your existing offer.
  - Brand pillars. Remember, this is about creating an experience, and the brand pillars are its foundation. Develop three brand pillars that help guide all decision-making in the future for operations, products, and design. Brand pillars help guide our design if we want to be thought of as local or we

want to our products delivered with speed. These are examples of brand pillars that help define what the concept will stand for. Brand pillars are directional in nature, and the majority of decisions should follow them accordingly. It is important that your brand pillars are differentiating and that you can deliver on the expectations they establish.

- Vet your brand pillars with customers
  - Focus groups. Now is the time to determine whether the brand pillars resonate with your prospective and existing customers. Bouncing ideas off customers in a focus group is an excellent way to vet your pillars. If you are spot on, that is great news. If there is pushback, it's better to find that out now than later. If possible, get a cross sample of customers who are loyal to your brand and those who visit your stores intermittently.
  - Intercepts. Customer intercepts are another way to get feedback on products and brand design. Speaking to existing customers engages real-life users of your current designs and potentially excites your customer base that good things are coming.
  - Surveys. Online surveys allow the most participation by your followers on social media and get your customers to participate in the process. Sometimes the best ideas come from the people who use your services.
- Manage the myriad of decisions
  - Assign a gatekeeper. All decisions should flow through one person. Note that I didn't say that this gatekeeper makes all the decisions, but he or she should manage the decision-making process. This is a critical role in keeping all parties on task.
  - Establish a cross-functional team. Cross-functional teams involved in all key aspects of the business are critical to the long-term success. The team should include people from operations, merchandising, real estate, and marketing. Better to get them involved sooner rather than have them second-guess you later.

- Don't underestimate the need for external expertise. Expertise from the outside brings fresh and often non-industry ideas to the table in addition to relieving the overload of tasks that have to be tackled by the internal team. Remember, your internal team members all have day jobs, and managing a complex strategic project in addition to their normal daily tasks can be very difficult. Also, this is not easy and often requires professional expertise. The expertise you engage should be able to help with establishing the brand strategy (brand pillars); two-dimensional items (e.g., store graphics, packaging); and three-dimensional items (architecture, store planning, interiors, colors and materials selection, etc.).
- Store attributes dictate size. Most approaches consist of picking a store and then filling it with merchandising. An alternative approach is to identify all the attributes (food, beer, etc.) that will be a part of the store, and base the size of the store on the number of attributes.

Manage the art

Managing the art requires the same type of rigor as the overall management of the process. Brand design should be functional as well as attractive. Without efficiency and operational considerations, the brand design will be difficult to maintain as it is extended to multiple store configurations.

- Build on the brand pillars
  - Brand architecture to support. The entire family of brand elements should work with your brand pillars. Nomenclature, fonts, colors, and branding hierarchy should create a cohesive branding package.
  - Develop key signature items that are in concert with the brand pillars. This is critical to giving customers an easy way of remembering the core elements of your brand. You may think and sleep your brand, but your customers don't—a signature offer makes it easy for them to remember you.

- Integrate the brand vertically. All communication elements in the store should speak toward the brand. This means that the visual (what you look like), the verbal (how you talk about yourself), and the behavioral (how you act) all need to be aligned so as to communicate and reinforce a cohesive brand message and experience.
- From uniforms to paper products to how employees engage the customer, all these branding components working in unison help solidify the brand. It only takes one negative interaction with a store employee to tarnish your brand.
- Store design and flow
  - Standardize your template. No two stores are built alike, so developing a standardized template to which modifications and adaptations can be made is critical to the management of the brand.
  - Modify to other store types. From the standardized template, create prototypical layouts that represent the array of store sizes in your network.
- Testing and validation
  - Test the prototype. Expect to build a prototype and tweak the next several stores; it is the nature of the beast. Gaining real-life feedback from the customer is absolutely critical to fine-tuning your brand.
  - Seek post-open consumer feedback. Formally surveying both new and existing customers on the new concept helps provide an alternate perspective to the overall experience.
  - There are no silver bullets. It is critical to go into this process with an open mind, as there are many ways to express your brand design. There are no silver bullets—brand design and operational expression of that design are two of the many factors that contribute to the success of a store.

Strategic branding projects like creating a store of the future are immensely complex, will drain internal resources, and take nonstop effort to keep on task. They can be quite daunting to tackle, straining even the best organizations and taxing their daily operations. But in the end, strategic branding communicates the future of your chain to your customers as well as becoming a rallying cry for your entire organization.

Operational Excellence

Managing a retail store is tough work.

Between operations, merchandising, marketing, and facility upkeep, retail business owners have their hands full. Managing the details of retail is the difference between success and failure. All too often, retail owners become lax in their operation and put themselves at an unnecessary disadvantage with their customers. It may seem elementary, yet so many retailers miss the little things—the details that customers notice. They miss the chance to be operationally excellent.

Retail is the process of managing the details to allow for what is extremely beneficial—taking care of the customer. I am sure many of you have walked into a retail store to find the employees too busy with operational items to help customers. That shows a lack of preplanning and operational execution that should have been completed well in advance of a customer walking into the store. Being operationally excellent requires developing systems and procedures to address all the little details of running your store, many of which are transparent to the customer. The only time that these details become apparent to the customer is when they are not addressed.

Being operationally excellent enables your employees to transcend being employees to become ambassadors of your store. When employees become ambassadors of the store and its personality, they become an extension of the brand image. Operational excellence requires you to think through every detail of your operation and develop a plan for each area in advance of customer interaction, allowing for friendly and successful customer service. In the end, your employees and customers will benefit from the following:

Train your team

Detailing your expectations of your team in advance is one way to ensure that each employee is cross-trained and aware of his or her role in the store. All too often, managers leave procedures to chance, and employees will take the path of least resistance, often shortchanging the customer. Identifying and mapping the procedures for your team's success in advance provides both the employee and the customer the optimal experience.

Make your marketing more powerful

Investing money in marketing is critical to any successful business. If you are like most retailers, making your local marketing more efficient is paramount. There is nothing more frustrating than communicating a motivating marketing campaign to drive in customer traffic, then dropping the ball operationally. Not only does this waste money, but it also most likely chases away customers who will never return. Your operation has to be impeccable about delivering on marketing promises.

Deliver better customer service

Customers are busy people. While you might like to believe that customers enjoy standing in line or waiting for a sales associate to greet them, the truth of the matter is that many would rather buy and go. Having your operation in tip-top shape not only delivers the best service to each customer, but also increases the number of customers you can reach. I am not suggesting a robotic approach, but rather an interaction that leaves the customer feeling confident in your operation.

Improve operational throughput

Creating a work environment that is focused and organized provides the opportunity to take advantage of incremental sales that come your way. In a disorganized retail setting, customers will become impatient and seek other options—i.e., your competition. Your goal is to capture every sales opportunity that comes into your store, and if your operation is humming along, these additional sales will fold in seamlessly. Every operational procedure put in place should be created in order to increase throughput.

Build energy and focus

Employees who have clear direction and roles will channel their energy toward greater customer service rather than spending time trying to figure out what is expected of them. In my experience, operational teams have always been able to take on significantly more if expectations were fair and focused. Spending time up front with your team will pay handsome dividends in their development and customer service.

Provide balance

Let's face it: we work because we have to. Given the choice between scrubbing baseboards and lying by the pool, almost all of us would choose the latter. While we cannot afford to live the life of luxury 100 percent of the time, managing our workplaces to ensure the most efficient operation possible is the optimal scenario to maintaining balance in our lives. Creating an excellent operational work environment enables you to surpass the expectations of your operations while providing for a healthy work/life balance.

In retail, it is the little items that add up—operations are about preparation first, then execution. Having your store buttoned up from top to bottom not only puts your best foot forward to your customers, but also ensures that your entire staff is in alignment with your expectations. Consistency and execution will take your store further and be harder for your competition to replicate. Focus like a laser on operational excellence, and you will see a steady increase in sales.

The Art of Execution

Retailers talk the talk, but often miss on walking the walk. Operational excellence has a singular focus: the customer. The customer is treated as a privilege, not a right, and his or her patronage needs to be earned daily. With that in mind, every process, every step, every task that is executed in the store has to have the customer in mind.

The art of execution is a discipline that elevates the retailer in the eyes of its customers not as a place to visit on occasion, but as a place to seek out. This cult-like persona that a retailer can achieve with its patrons requires that the entire staff be in lockstep alignment to cater to the needs of the customer. This level of execution applies to all facets of the operation, from service to merchandise to cleanliness to everything.

Create an overachieving mind-set with your staff, and the energy will be contagious. This attention to detail and putting the customer first will enable the retailer to ride out even the worst economic storms. Execution should be precise and an attention to detail that is second to none.

Management sets the tone
It all begins here. If management is 100 percent engaged, this mind-set can permeate and cascade throughout the entire team. Operational excellence has a fighting chance, and the art of execution can be flawless. A management staff that is in it at only 80 percent conveys this to the staff, and if the staff is only capturing 80 percent of the 80 percent, operational excellence quickly deteriorates. Management is the driver; success means leading by example.

Pay attention to details
Why sweat the details? Because that is where the customer is converted from occasional patron to passionate ambassador. Knowing their names, keeping merchandise in stock, neatly kept displays, cleanliness on all levels, a smile from your staff—all executional details that create a customer for life. Customers have options—look for the proprietary details that you can communicate and execute on in order to lock in your customers.

Go to the customer

Making the effort to overachieve in your store is one thing; taking your execution to your three-mile radius and cultivating your customer base is quite another thing. Going to your customers and making their experience all the more convenient will solidify their admiration for you. While you may not be set up to delivery or provide mobile services on a regular basis, going the extra mile in one-off situations may be the detail that captivates a neighbor or town. The goal is to make the customer experience as memorable and effortless as possible.

Customize your suggestive sell

Link together items that help your customers connect the dots with regard to their needs, not yours. A retailer that masters the art of selling suggestively in a way that empowers the customer has found a winning scenario. I am not suggesting some rote recital of "Would you like some fries with that?" but rather a customized interaction with the customer that addresses his or her exact needs. Create this mutually beneficial relationship with your best customers, and your competitors will be shaking in their boots.

Appreciate your patrons

Lastly, the art of execution is built on one premise: the customer is a privilege, not a right. Cater to your customers; treat them as guests in your home, and your relationships with them will run deep. If you view customers as interruptions to your daily routine—"Damn, I need to take care of this customer"—and they will, in turn, treat your store like the commodity you project. Any customers you can transform into ambassadors for your brand will translate into ongoing success for many years to come.

Labor Management

Labor management is one of the fundamental aspects of running a profitable business. Service the customer with too few people on staff, and sales will be negatively affected, as customers will shop elsewhere. Staff the business with too many people, and profits will be lost to labor expense. The key to managing labor is finding the sweet spot where customer service is met with the appropriate number of labor dollars spent.

Building a labor schedule is no easy task, and managing it requires constant oversight. In order to run a business, you need to establish a minimum baseline to keep it operating. If you are in the retail business, obviously at least one person needs to be in the store at all times. Beyond the minimum baseline, most companies view labor as a percentage of sales—i.e., if sales increase, labor expense increases proportionally. This type of management allows the business to adjust the schedule.

The ebb and flow of labor management takes into account all seasonal, geographic, and business demands. Prudent managers know how to schedule according to year-over-year results, influences of marketing, and what is required to provide excellent customer service. Here are some key items to consider when creating a labor-management schedule:

Number of people required

The first step is to determine how many people you need on the staff. Not all employees will be working at the same time, so you will have to understand the dynamics of each employee. Employees may be paid different wages, have more time available to work, and be trained in different skill sets. The manager needs to mesh all these attributes together to determine the optimal weekly schedule.

Labor dollars versus budget

Once the manager is cognizant of all the employee nuances regarding scheduling, he or she can begin to build a budget. The budget may be an annual labor target cost to begin with, but it is then more finely defined based on seasonality and trends. Once the budget has been established, it will help determine the other key drivers of labor that include wage rates, number of hours scheduled, and overtime allotment. Those drivers are the keys to managing your weekly budget.

Wage rate—manager, assistant, and crew

Setting guidelines for wage rates for all your positions is critical. Over time, these wage rates will change with cost-of-living adjustments and performance. Take into account the skill set and wage rate of each staff member in order to optimize labor costs. Highly productive employees generally garner the highest wages. The tradeoff is that these highly skilled employees can manage their jobs more efficiently, which allows the manager to run the store with fewer staff members. The balancing act of productivity versus wage rate is the key.

Ceiling hours

The number of hours allocated to be used are known as ceiling hours. Setting a schedule based on anticipated sales volume is the first step in establishing ceiling hours. Every manager should know the corresponding labor hours for sales volume, based on a blended hourly wage. The blended hourly wage rate is determined by combining the number of hours each employee is working. If ceiling hours are exceeded, not only will labor be over budget, but also the amount may be further increased due to overtime.

Overtime

Run your operation too tightly—without contingencies for incremental business—and you may find that you have to invest more in overtime than anticipated. Generating extra business is a great issue to have, but watching the incremental profits being eroded by overtime is not. The shrewd operator manages his or her labor with the right amount of slack in the schedule to adjust to customer demands without having to pay a premium.

Turnover—manager, assistant, and crew

Lastly, managing turnover—in particular of highly skilled, cross-trained employees—is paramount for the long-term management of labor. Continual turnover at a business requires a disproportionate amount of labor to train new employees rather than service customers. Every employee who is lost—especially if he or she is capable—can negatively affect management of top-line sales increases.

Labor management is a balancing act. If you have wage rates under control but spend a disproportionate amount on overtime, your wage rate will increase dramatically. Balancing your labor to service the customer requires continual monitoring and cross training of your core staff to ensure that productivity matches the investment.

The Basics of Franchising

Upon opening his or her first store, many operators come to the often-premature decision to franchise. While this may be a noble goal, what is often missing is the determination of whether the concept is franchise-able. There are many questions that need to be answered, systems and procedures that need to be developed, and a myriad of other items to be addressed before one can venture off and franchise his or her concept.

The difference between a franchisor and franchisee is fairly obvious—the franchisor is the person who owns a company, along with its trademarks and products, while the franchisee is in charge of running an individual franchise. Potential franchisors have to address the following questions before moving forward with the plan to franchise:

- Will a franchisee be able to afford the operating expenses of your concept?
- Does the operating break-even analysis offset the royalty, ad fee, and other ongoing expenses for the franchisee?
- What products and/or services will be offered, and will they succeed in other locations?
- How steep is the learning curve for an inexperienced individual to understand and learn the business's concept?

What makes a franchise business attractive for an outsider is that the services and products are generally proven and have an established reputation, so the concept has been vetted. In addition, with incremental locations all sharing the same brand, costs for marketing, advertising, and launching the business are shared. Procurement costs should be lower, as more locations combine their purchasing power. Lastly, systems and procedures are mapped for the franchisee so that each individual can quickly be trained on how to go to market.

These are just a few of the items that can indicate if your concept is ready to be transformed into a franchise. If it is full steam ahead, then the following items need to be addressed:

Disclosure overview

Every franchise has to produce a franchise disclosure document (FDD) in order to legally offer franchises. The FDD must disclose a number of items for potential franchisees to review. First and foremost is an overall summary of the business and any potential competitors. Other items are regulatory compliance for the industry, the background and litigation history of the franchisor, information on trademark registrations, investment expectations for the franchisee, and the franchisor's audited financials. Essentially, the FDD provides the pertinent background of the potential franchisee's future partner.

Franchisor duties

The franchisor has the duty not only to support the overall franchise, but also to provide support to the individual franchisees. A franchise is only as strong as the collective strength of the franchisees. Therefore, the franchisor needs to maintain a solid organization that continually grows the enterprise with new franchisees and locations. In addition, once the franchisees are established, the franchisor is responsible for training and supporting the franchisees, managing the overall brand, and outsourcing products and services for the company. Lastly, the franchisor is obligated to manage and maintain the integrity of the market areas and territories of stores.

Franchisor key decisions

Now you have to get down to the cold, hard facts—what to charge! Generally, every franchise has an initial franchise fee as well as ongoing royalties. In some cases, multiple franchise locations may allow for a reduction in the initial franchise fee. Royalty payments are calculated on a percentage of sales. In addition, in order to maintain the integrity of the franchise, certain suppliers will be authorized for use by the franchisees. The franchisor also needs to determine what ongoing support and training will be provided and disclose this in the FDD. Lastly, the franchisor should determine the ongoing advertising contributions that will be charged to the franchisees.

Franchisor responsibilities—preopening

The work doesn't stop for the franchisor once the franchisee is on board. Prior to opening, the franchisor generally helps the franchisee select a site and in some cases, negotiate a lease. It is in the franchisor's best interest to attract franchisees that are positioned for success with "A" locations. Once the site is selected, training the franchisee staff on systems and procedures is next, to ensure that processes at the store level will not deviate significantly from the original concept. Lastly, prior to opening, the franchisor should assist with product procurement, store build-out, and development of a plan for opening.

Franchisor responsibilities—post-opening

After the store is open, the franchisor should have a routine to ensure that the franchisee is complying with all programs. Creating a vibrant brand for the enterprise remains paramount for the franchisor as he or she manages and implements the ad fund. Once critical mass is achieved, sharing this stewardship with a franchise advisory committee (FAC) and gaining its input in advance ensures greater success for ad campaigns. Lastly, as with all well-run agreements, holding both parties accountable for their contract obligations creates a long-lasting, mutually beneficial arrangement.

The decision to franchise should not be taken lightly. If your concept is unique and its financial success can be transferred to another owner for the benefit of both parties, then the franchise has legs. All too often, store operators who want to franchise do not have the appropriate levels of discipline and control in place in advance. This is a disservice not only to the franchisor, but also to the franchisee.

Franchise Advisory Councils

Establishing a franchise advisory council (FAC) as a formal communications system for franchisee input on marketing and operations is a natural stepping-stone for a growing franchise operation. FAC representatives are an indispensable part of the communication system in that they help represent the franchise. The FAC is charged with garnering input, questions, and suggestions from franchisees in their area and communicating this to the corporation. In the council meetings, representatives share these ideas and questions with other representatives and members of the staff. It is crucial to note, though, that the FAC doesn't replace one-to-one communication between franchisees and the company staff. Rather, it should augment, encourage, and enhance communication on all levels by providing an opportunity for direct franchisee input.

The pros and cons of establishing a FAC, as well as the process, are outlined below. On balance, the advantages outweigh the disadvantages for most franchise systems, and FACs are critical to evolving relationships between the company and its franchisees.

Key advantages

This council establishes lines of communication between the franchise community and the franchisor. It provides input from franchisees with regard to systems, procedures, products, and services, as well as how the franchise system operates. This establishes an ongoing dialogue between franchisee representatives (the FAC) and the parent company. The FAC is the sounding board for new concepts and ideas that allow the franchisor to judge the effectiveness of a program in advance of a system-wide rollout. The franchisor seeks the endorsement of the FAC before launching an initiative to the entire system. All in all, a well-run FAC can establish more harmonious communications between the franchisor and its franchisees.

Key disadvantages

Management by committee is one of the key dangers of establishing a FAC. A poorly managed FAC may cause the company to lose control of the overall direction of the franchise and become disjointed in its focus by acquiescing to special interests as opposed to the broader base. In addition, the overall selection and makeup of the FAC will have a significant impact on its effectiveness. Since the FAC is generally selected through a democratic voting process, disgruntled franchisees will have a vastly different impact than satisfied franchisees. Lastly, both the company and the FAC should be aware of antitrust laws.

FAC member duties

FAC members are representatives of the overall franchisee community and are expected to seek and communicate the views of their constituents. While they may have opinions regarding the decisions of the company, it is rare that they can veto a program presented by the franchisor. However, it is in the best interest of the franchisor to actively seek the endorsement of the FAC on all rollout decisions. FAC members are expected to cover such topics as operations, advertising, goods and services, equipment, communications, and corporate policy.

FAC nomination process

Typically, the process of electing FAC members is as follows:

- Each store submits a nominating ballot, listing as many as three candidates. This list may include the franchisee.
- Only those in good standing with the company should be eligible.

- Where franchisees are spouses, either spouse would be eligible for nomination.
- The nominees must have been operating their stores for a length of time determined by the franchisor.
- The candidates with the most votes should be notified and asked if they accept the nomination.
- The candidates who accept nomination are listed on the ballot.

FAC member attributes

FAC representatives need to be good listeners in order to gather input from other franchisees. They must be able to combine those ideas, along with their own experiences, into constructive suggestions for improvement in a competitive marketplace. Obviously, they must also maintain their good standing with the franchisor throughout their tenure.

Frequency of meetings

The franchise advisory council should meet approximately once every quarter, with communication ongoing throughout the year. In addition, the franchisor typically schedules a social event or outing each year. Agenda items need to be communicated in advance in order for FAC members to effectively seek field input.

In summary, a well-managed FAC can yield a tremendous opportunity for the franchisor and franchisees to work as one. This process of two-way communication helps to foster excellent franchise relations and provides the franchisor with another collective set of eyes for new product development, effective marketing, and field support. While the FAC may provide an effective sounding board for the company, it is a critical that the franchisor continues to communicate with franchisees on an individual level. This ongoing individual communication combined with the involvement of the FAC provides a cohesive relationship among all parties.

GrayCat
Enterprises, Inc.

CHAPTER 4

MERCHANDISING

The Keys to Merchandising

Merchandising is a critical aspect of how shoppable a store will be. Conceal merchandise or confuse the customer, and it won't matter if you carry the top brands; the customer will become frustrated and leave the store. Many retailers simply stack it high and let it fly without considering the nuances of proper merchandising.

By guiding customers through your store with their favorite products easily accessible, you have an excellent opportunity to turn inventory over more quickly and thus increase profits. Failing to provide the top products due to out-of-stocks or through cluttered merchandising will frustrate them.

The goal of a merchandising strategy is to make the shopping experience quick, efficient, and easy for the customer. While some customers may wish to take their time shopping the store, let that be *their* choice, not something forced on them by poor merchandising. Let's take a look at some specifics:

Display area

A clearly delineated display area helps guide customers to merchandise, allowing for easy shopping and, ultimately, purchasing. Merchandising can be highlighted with specific store designs and gondolas. All too often, retailers cram products onto shelves without rhyme or reason and expect the customer to navigate them for their purchases. The set and display should make it easy for the customer to say yes.

Fixtures

Fixtures should be used to accentuate the merchandise, not conceal it. Select fixtures that allow the product to be showcased and easily stocked. Fixtures that are too high prevent inviting sight lines as well as creating a security risk. Dark, dingy, and filthy fixtures detract from the products.

Merchandise

Of course, selecting the most consumer-preferred merchandise is critical to the overall success of your store. Category management strategies call for the appropriate number of SKUs for the fastest-moving items and the premium position on the fixtures. Out-of-stocks will not only hurt the immediate sale, but also cast doubt on whether the store can be trusted to have a customer's favorite brands on his or her next visit. In some cases, it only takes one out-of-stock experience to lose a customer.

Plan-o-grams

Every product should have a predetermined placement on the merchandising fixture. A plan-o-gram is a tool that visually communicates the placement and pricing of products within the category and/or fixture. Haphazardly placing products leaves profits on the shelves instead of in the register.

Pricing

Pricing should be considered within a holistic, store strategy. In particular, if multiple employees are making pricing decisions, be careful to ensure that not everything in the store is on sale. A collective pricing strategy enables a retailer to drive volume with certain products while protecting margin with others. Success lies in the combination of both of these approaches so that the store optimizes revenue and profits.

Signage

Signage is a crucial element, providing both directional messaging and price points. It is critical that signage not be overwhelmingly busy or so plentiful that the store becomes a cacophony of messaging. Customers need to be guided through the store rather than inundated with over communication.

Product adjacencies

Placing products that are complementary next to one another increases the average ticket sale of the store. If you are selling shirts, having ties next to them is an excellent example of product-adjacency strategy. Stores that fail to link products with adjacency placement miss out on sales and profits.

Category Management Process

With the start of each year, planning for your annual merchandising and promotional schedule should be in place. For the multiunit operator, identifying the key initiatives for each merchandising category is critical to remaining on plan and on budget throughout the year. Each category should have targeted initiatives, all represented with sales and margin goals—including rebates—with assigned owners and key deadlines identified.

All too often, multiunit operators leave too much to chance with their merchandising or simply promote items from month to month without a cohesive annualized plan. A well-thought-out category management plan enables the operator to know in advance where incremental sales and margin will come from.

Failure to create these initiatives with benchmark financial metrics will leave the retailer wallowing in missed opportunities throughout the year. Dovetailing these category targets with a monthly key performance initiatives (KPI) review will assist in keeping the plan on time and on budget.

Productivity initiatives

Each of these initiatives should be a productivity task—in other words, achieving results through noncapital investments. Identify a series of initiatives for each category and the amount of sales, margin, and rebates you expect. Identify initiatives in each category that will add to the previous year's baseline. Initiatives should include both growth initiatives as well and offsets (price increases, etc.).

Core store plans

Initiatives developed by category roll up to new yearly sales, margin, and rebate projections. This exercise holds the category manager accountable for financial expectations as well as on-time delivery. The key is to be able to identify all the growth tasks for the category and to implement them in a timely fashion.

Growth/acquisition store plans

If you prefer, the operator can bifurcate the initiatives into baseline stores (core) and new stores (growth or acquisitions). This enables the owner to determine if growth at the core or base-store level is because of productivity or simply adding more stores.

Key owner

Initiatives are assigned an owner and a deadline for implementation. Ongoing operations meetings should include discussion of past implementation and next-quarter initiatives, including post analyses. This keeps the category team from missing deadlines, projections, and implementation steps. The post-analysis process puts in place a discipline that can be used to vet future ideas with concrete benchmarks.

Time table

Lastly, all initiatives should have specific launch and completion dates. Remember, the financial targets and expectations of each task are predicated on this. In other words, missing the dates that financial expectations are due to begin puts the achievement of those metrics in peril.

At the end of the day, each category should have a number of key initiatives identified and projects planned for implementation throughout the year. The monthly KPI review process generates financial updates on the status of each. Make adjustments to ensure that financial goals are met. By establishing these plans in advance, the multiunit operator can prosper throughout the year with a cohesive category strategy.

Developing a Winning Food-Service Strategy

With a constant blurring of retail lines, some forward-thinking operators are attempting to diversify by introducing food-service items in their stores. Most facilities provide plenty of customer traffic and space to enable modifications for a food-service operation. While the desire to incorporate food service is in the forefront, operators need to address every aspect of the implementation.

With the appropriate modifications to their operational systems and procedures, retail owners can slowly unveil a food-service offering. Make a concerted effort to market outside the store to attract new customers, capitalizing on improved merchandising and signage and developing better metrics and KPIs. Only through a holistic approach can stores be poised for a giant leap forward to improved profitability.

Overall business planning

It is essential to understand the direction of both retail stores and food-service operations. Separating the food-service component from the rest of the P&L will enable a true assessment of the operation. For ease of computing, labor can be an estimated allocated number of hours. By doing this, you can see if the operation is performing adequately using a break-even analysis and four-wall analysis. In addition, any CAPEX improvements can be reviewed for ROI, and each of these reports can be rolled up into a three-year pro forma.

Operational excellence

Food-service operations are viewed differently than typical retail establishments from an accounting standpoint. The big three in food service are food, paper, and labor. Tied to inventory management, this is the only way to manage food service. Systems and procedures are then built to support the overall management of operations. Food-service operators leave nothing to chance and develop metrics and procedures in a disciplined fashion to regularly monitor the business. Prepare for opportunity.

Merchandising and in-store promotion

All quick-service restaurants (QSRs) utilize some sort of value or combo meal. Take the time to develop and market combos to help customers decide on items, improve speed of operation, and raise ticket averages. That being said, out-of-stocks need to be nonexistent, and merchandising should utilize product placement adjacencies. These complementary items are developed to capture all opportunities. Potential shortfalls can be easily avoided through systems and procedures, and addressing them improves sales and margins.

Local store marketing and advertising plans

Cultivation of customers, both onsite and offsite, is generally nonexistent in retail industries, but not in the fast and casual food markets. Window signage with product photography is a must, and outside local store marketing opportunities need to be put in place. Overall signage needs a whole new approach to guide and entice customers. Opportunities in catering and to-go marketing are plentiful and require a proactive plan. All marketing activities should be included in an annual advertising plan.

Key performance indicators

Knowing the key drivers is the only way to improve a business's bottom line. Lumping the food-service results in with the retail product P&L

makes it difficult to understand the nuances of food service. A series of KPIs should be developed in order to determine where the opportunities exist and provide the steps toward improvements. Conducting a marketing/operational pilot is a key step in creating the benchmarks to target.

Vendor management and purchasing

Vendor management is important for both retail and food-service operations. Managing your vendor drop-off times is critical (i.e., not having totes stacked in front of food service at 11:45 a.m.). In addition, inventory management at the store level with regard to FIFO (first in, first out) is not only smart, it is food safe. Food service means you need to be aligned with the right vendors who can help you expand your operation in tandem with the customer needs; it cannot be a deterrent.

Launching a food-service operation in your retail store is both an exciting initiative and a smart decision. Manage it correctly and you enjoy the benefits of high-margin products that address the growing customer need of improved food-service items. On the flip side, run your food-service operation like a typical retail store and you will be disappointed with the results.

Vendor Management and Alignment

Aligning vendors to a common business vision is a daunting task. In many cases, vendors for retail outlets number in the hundreds, if not thousands. How can the retailer manage all of them? The key is to take control and focus the vendors on *your* business vision, not theirs. The retailer must lead, rather than be led.

This does not mean to ride roughshod over your vendors, but rather to point them in the correct direction along with other vendors. When the vendor community aligns with a common vision, it clearly allows for a rising tide that lifts all boats. Retailers who can pull off this feat are blessed with the benefits of competition and its impact on driving sales. Vendors that know the retailer's endgame can bring more aligned resources to their category and ultimately grow their brands.

So how does a retailer pull off this task of vendor alignment? I am a big believer in a communication event that provides the platform to articulate a common business vision. I used to organize an annual autumn vendor conference that allowed our company to explain where we were headed in the upcoming year. Hundreds of vendors would attend this event and hear firsthand from the senior team what our financial and key initiative projections were for the upcoming year. Vendors were asked to participate and invest in the initiatives in order to achieve these goals. This annual event grew each and every year and provided a format for efficient communication for both the retailer and the vendors.

Align to a common vision
The key is alignment with your vendors. An annual vendor conference provides a platform to inform, educate, and align your vendors for the upcoming year. Vendors get to hear the vision firsthand and consistent from the senior team. Questions are answered, and plan details are articulated. The vendors who attend are in the know and have a leg up on vendors who do not.

Force your team to plan
From an internal standpoint, the annual vendor conference creates a budget and planning deadline that your team must meet in order to be effective at the event. This hard deadline is usually ahead of when most retailers complete their annual planning. In our case, I always liked to conduct our annual conference in October—either a few weeks before or after the national industry convention. This allowed our team to use the national convention as a secondary communication avenue with our vendors by either prepping them for our upcoming conference or finalizing plans that began with our annual event.

Apply peer pressure

There is nothing better than having competing vendors in the same audience, hearing a business vision and determining how they will outflank one another. This peer pressure is gold for the retailer, since it puts him or her in the best possible negotiating stance with vendors. Representatives from the sales level to senior management will want to ensure that their companies are well represented in your plans throughout the upcoming year.

Negotiate while in the zone

Feel the vision and act on the vision. When the vendors are all hyped up after the senior management presentations, it is time to close the deal. The expectation that the annual conference is where deals get made should be set in advance, and vendors should be ready to sign on the dotted line. Clearly, this is a negotiating tactic for the retailer, but more importantly, it creates a sense of urgency to finalize vendor commitments, allowing for a focus on executing those plans. There is no reason to delay this process unless you are woefully unprepared.

Senior management attracts senior management

Your top brass will attract your vendor's top brass. Use the draw of access to your senior team to attract the senior teams of your vendors. The more aligned you are with the senior management at your vendors, the more attention—and resources—will come your way. Sell the senior management and access to programs, and incremental budgets will soon follow.

Invest dollars for returns

An annual vendor conference is a critical strategy that not only aligns your vendors but also provides a sense of urgency for your team to plan for the upcoming year. While there are dollars to be invested to court and entertain vendors, the resulting impact of an efficient platform is substantial in the return of investment from your vendors. The squeaky wheel gets the oil, and if you can pull off a well-orchestrated annual vendor conference, the investment will return handsomely.

Vendor RFP Process

We select our store locations. We select our staff. We select the merchandise to carry, and along those lines, we select our vendors. Selecting the correct vendors—in addition to managing these vendors during the selection process and beyond—can often be the difference between making your store profitable and simply providing real estate for the vendors to sell their goods. It is time to manage your vendors!

Raise your hand if you have ever conducted a thorough request for proposal (RFP) process for your vendors. Anyone? In truth, not many have to the extent that they evaluate multiple vendors, creating competition for space in their stores. How you manage the RFP process can and will set the tone for all your go-forward vendors. A well-thought-out vendor selection process can provide real opportunities for you in the following areas:

Rebates

Did you know that vendors offer rebates based on product placement, rack allowances, product movement, and other considerations? In some cases, the vendor receives manufacturing rebates that you need to ensure are passed on to you. The RFP process ensures that you identify and capture your fair share.

Incentives

Vendors are in your store for one thing—to sell their products. You should only meet the goals of the vendors if they are aligned with your goals. What types of incentives do your vendors provide in order to meet their goals? Work with the vendor to establish incentives for each party that foster alignment.

Deliveries

You pay for delivery whether you believe that or not. Manage the number of weekly deliveries to your store so that you have enough inventory on hand, but not so much that you are paying full-load delivery fees for partial deliveries. You may want to consider adjustments based on seasonality.

Never out of basics

All stores carry must-have products that you can never be out of—ever! Identify your must-have products and ensure that your vendors have a clear understanding of the consequences if any of these products are ever out of stock. Build in financial penalties for the vendor if you are shorted product on your core offerings.

Marketing

Identify programs and investments that your vendor partners will make in advertising and promoting their products. These should be managed in concert with your overall store marketing and determined jointly with the vendors to ensure their financial obligation, as well as timing.

Payment terms

Standard policy is net thirty days, but have you inquired about discounts if you pay earlier? If you are in a position to negotiate more favorable payment terms, do so.

Product returns

Have you established a specific contractual obligation on product returns and damages? Restocking fees and other incremental markups on returned products by your vendor could eat away at your profits. In addition, now is the time to establish the process for replacing damaged products.

Contract terms

How long are you committed to this vendor, and what are the out clauses in the contract should a better vendor come along? The best place to negotiate this is during the RFP process when the vendor is hungry for your business.

Markups

Every product you purchase comes with a corresponding markup—the manufacturer/vendor profit. Most of these markups are determined by the category of products rather than the product SKU. Knowing your industry markup ranges by category will better prepare you to establish the best cost structure for your products.

Conducting a thorough RFP process is critical not only for establishing your pricing structure with your vendors but also for developing the process by which business is conducted. Remember, vendors are in *your* store, and it is up to you to determine the role that each of them plays. If you do not take control of your vendors from the onset, you will face an uphill battle. Or as Winston Churchill once said, "He who fails to plan is planning to fail."

GrayCat
Enterprises, Inc.

CHAPTER 5

MARKETING

Effective Branding: Beyond the Logo

Marketers of retail stores have a common goal—they are constantly working to strengthen their store brand. They know brand power translates into increased sales. A store's brand is more than just a logo—it represents all that the company stands for. Today's store marketers are faced with more challenges in promoting their brands than their predecessors twenty years ago, but fortunately, they are armed with far better strategic branding tools than ever before.

Successful branding is based on a number of must-haves. The consumer needs to be offered a promise by or expectation of the brand, branding needs to help the consumer identify and relate to the store, and a store's brand must set it apart from its competition. Branding helps cement an emotional bond with customers. In the past, successful branding was achieved solely through a brand-centric approach—putting the brand first and foremost. But as technology continues to advance, companies are now putting the customer at the forefront of their efforts, often incorporating consumer-centric strategies into their branding efforts as well.

Brand-centric strategies cast a big net: you create a brand, build some stores, and then communicate with potential customers in a large area via mass advertising in print, on the radio, on billboards and on television. Billions of dollars are spent annually on mass marketing, and those dollars helped shape some of the biggest, most recognized brands in America. Unfortunately, it is often difficult to measure the results of mass marketing as an ongoing strategy.

Don't throw out brand-centric just yet

Brand-centric strategies are still very much a part of today's marketing arsenal as they provide the broad reach required to move large groups of consumers. An example of brand-centric marketing is when a store chain buys radio advertisements. The message reaches far and wide, touting the brand without addressing individual customer needs, but rather geographically targeting stores that have proven to respond well to advertising. Sophisticated marketers help further target potential customers by employing brand development indices (BDI): measurement tools to minimize advertising-dollar waste. BDIs identify specific stores that respond better than others to advertising, based on sales. It is the fish-where-the-fish-are-biting theory—spending ad dollars where they deliver the greatest returns.

One example of ill-fated brand-centric marketing strategy occurred with the Oldsmobile brand. In 1985, Oldsmobile had a 6.9 percent market share in the automobile sector, but GM recognized that its Oldsmobile customer base was aging. In an effort to attract a younger customer base to Olds, GM changed the brand's proclamation to "This is not your father's Oldsmobile." The company led its marketing efforts with a repositioning of the brand and delivered this slogan through mass media. By 2000, Oldsmobile's market share had plummeted to 1.6 percent, and General Motors phased out Olds.

What happened here? Brand marketers tried a brand-centric strategy that failed miserably because younger customers had no interest in the brand. Marketers thought simply changing the brand catchphrase would be enough to entice new, younger customers to the brand. GM would have been better off approaching this potential customer base with a brand more tailored to its needs and desires rather than trying to reposition a legacy brand. It failed to recognize that it needed its existing customers to stay and that new ones needed to be cultivated differently.

Hello, consumer-centric

The new branding approach is consumer-centric—win a customer once, keep him or her for life. Consumer-centric strategies enable the company to have a one-on-one relationship with a customer in a customized, cost-efficient way—enabling the brand to keep that customer through all his or her life changes. Apple is an excellent example of this type of consumer-centric branding. Apple doesn't sell you a computer; it creates a one-on-one customer relationship with you. It achieves this by being large enough to wield the buying power yet nimble enough to build unique, customer-specific computers. This one-on-one customer relationship provides the perfect platform for Apple to keep its customers buying from them for the rest of their computing lives.

The field has leveled

The proliferation of social media, such as Facebook, Twitter, LinkedIn and YouTube, has enabled businesses of all sizes to establish and maintain ongoing relationships with their customers in a very affordable, informative, and entertaining fashion. Social media has leveled the playing field for smaller businesses to solidify a cult-like following among their customer base and efficiently communicate important information in real time. It is quite amazing how new companies can go to market in a cost-effective way and still deliver relevant content to their customer base.

One-on-one relationships

In today's branding world, savvy retail marketers need to focus their efforts on cultivating and maintaining customers through consumer-centric strategies such as customer relationship management (CRM) systems. These ongoing customer databases allow the company to establish customized, one-on-one customer communications and create loyalty programs, rewarding its best customers with special discounts and offers that cement their relationship with its brand. In addition, these multiplatform, one-to-one communication modes allow the business to communicate with customers on social media platforms, on its website, and via e-mail.

Each of these consumer-centric programs helps eliminate wasted marketing dollars while solidifying customers' loyalty. Retail store marketers who implement consumer-centric strategies will find that customers who are with them today will, more importantly, also be with them tomorrow.

Brand Positioning—A Focus on Clarity
Who are we?

That is a question I hear all the time from companies that are trying to better communicate with their customers. All too often, companies have grown in spite of not really knowing who they are or what they stand for. Rather, the growth has been derived through a series of bolt-on tactics without the presence of a strategic action plan that supports solid brand positioning. In the end, without this guiding force, companies find that their brands are disjointed and fail to capitalize fully on consumer opportunities.

While it would have been terrific foresight to have this guiding brand in place on day one, the reality is that a brand often needs to take a test drive in the marketplace for a bit in order to vet its acceptance. With that in mind, any company in business today can still tighten up its strategic vision and brand position. The goal is to capture what lies at the heart of this brand, what makes it compelling to consumers, and how it can become even stronger. If successful, a company can crystallize a shared, intuitive understanding of its brand and communicate more effectively to its customers.

Embarking on this process can be fun. Through a series of meetings, questionnaires, and customer intercepts, members of your team can see the brand unfold before their very eyes. Including a wider range of participants from office to store personnel can provide a wide swath of perceptions that all need to be considered in order to determine the best path forward for the brand. Add to that process some select front-line staff, and the branding development process should be complete. Done properly, the brand positioning exercise should not only identify where the company is today, but also to determine its vision for the future.

Garbage in, garbage out

This is similar to the chasing-the-shiny-penny syndrome, whereby long-term strategies change in a blink of an eye. Organizations without a properly vetted brand position often let market factors dictate where their brand is headed. While nimbleness can be a fantastic attribute for a company to possess, without guided structure, it creates a mishmash of branding messages and confusion for the customer. Before long, the guiding principles that once steered the company seem like a distant memory.

Describe your products/services

Start with the basics—the products. How would you describe the products you sell? Are they unique? Do they have some sort of special characteristic about them? If not, is your brand like all the rest? If so, how have you communicated the product attributes to your customers? Is it fast, clean, fresh, consistent, or large? Taking the time to identify the unique characteristics of your products helps differentiate your store from your competition.

What the products/services do for me

Next up, how are your products used, and what benefits do the customers derive from using them? Do your products make the customer happy and trouble free? Are the products helpful in the customer's life, or do they simply serve a means to an end? Perhaps the products save time. Extracting the benefits of the products and how they apply to your customer population emphasizes the uniqueness of your brand.

How the brand makes me look

Everyone wants to look good as well as smart in the choices they make in life. Walking around the city with a Starbucks cup carries a bit more status than drinking Folgers. Successful brands capture cult-like followings of which only those in the know are aware. The strength of cool crowd can carry the brand and its products a long way through a viral approach to brand building. These are the most competitively protected brands because they have capitalized on making their customers look good.

How the brand makes me feel

Similarly, how customers feel about your brand can propel your business forward significantly. When customers attribute to your brand and products an emotional connection and catalyst to their well being, you have a winner. Customers who feel energized and confident simply because of their interaction with your brand and products are customers for life. These customers will be ambassadors for the brand, and the benefits are immeasurable.

Strategic action plan

Lastly, after the brand essence has been identified, the objective of the strategic action plan is to create a detailed profile of what the company will look like in the future (products, consumers, geography, competition, financial performance, organization, etc.) and to identify the critical steps to achieving this profile. This will be the vehicle for the company to use in developing its operating plan, evolving its organizational structure, setting financial goals, determining which markets to enter and exit, and so on. Understanding your brand and its products will strengthen its longevity.

Brand Positioning—The Semantic Differential

One of the most interesting activities that I have been involved in regarding branding is called a semantic differential exercise. As discussed earlier, it is essential to provide clarity for the brand. It is important to delineate the attributes that form the brand and ensure that the business plans all point toward those attributes.

The semantic differential exercise is an excellent tool to help align those attributes not only for today, but also for where you want to steer the organization in the future. I particularly enjoy conducting this exercise with senior management teams to gauge how similarly the executives view the state of their brands. All too often, there are some glaring aha moments when the team is clearly disjointed on specific attributes.

Once the exercise is complete with the feedback from each team member, shoring up disparities for today as well as mapping tactics to move the organization toward the future can begin. Invariably, most leave the exercise with a sense of humbleness and humility. In the end, though, the steering attributes have been established, and the execution tactics may be developed.

The semantic differential asks the following question: "How would you describe the personality attributes of the brand in terms of how it is perceived today versus how it should be perceived in the future?" (Note: The dots are for demonstration purposes only.)

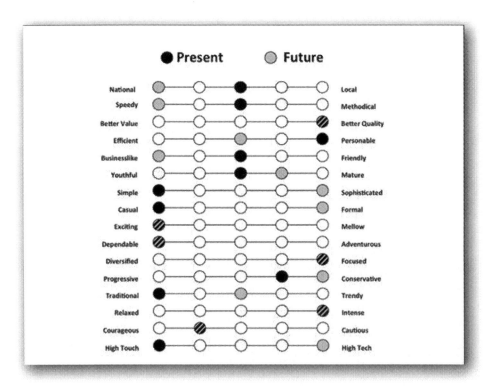

Determine opposing attributes

The attributes outlined can easily serve most brands. If you feel compelled to add more, consider attributes that are opposite each other, not necessarily the negatives of each other. Once the attributes are identified, each team member should complete a present and future chart for his or her feelings about the brand.

Reconcile the results

Next, consolidate the individual answers on the chart and come to a consensus on where the attributes are in the present as well as where the organization should steer them in the future. In some cases, the attributes may not need to move at all; in others, the disparity can be quite large.

Work the present, plan the future

With an aligned chart with both present and future attributes, now is the time to put them into action. Business plans that are developed for implementing tactics should be vetted against this chart for consistency. For large gaps, the action items may need to address multiple components from marketing to operations to culture and so on.

Be realistic

As with everything, the organization and the team need to be realistic. Sometimes the gaps are just too great to overcome. Kmart may aspire to become the next Tiffany, but realistically, that gap is way too wide. Organizations need to be aspirational with their brands, but within reason. It is quite OK to be a very operationally sound company that fits within your competency.

Revisit annually

Lastly, this shouldn't be a one-and-done. Reviewing the semantic differential annually is a healthy exercise to ensure that the organization is still on track. Aligning the senior team members on your overall branding will enable them to cascade directives that align with the future of the brand. Without clarity at the top, the message to the troops will be a muddy mess of noise in the field.

In summary, the semantic differential is an excellent communication tool that can translate some fairly abstract brand ideas into tangible directions. Using this chart as a guide, tactical implementations can be vetted against the steering attributes on an ongoing basis. Brand clarity is paramount for a company to keep on target and maximize the strength of its efforts.

Creating Your Branding Game Plan
What is your branding game plan?

Not the branding media schedule—that is just part of it—but rather, your overarching strategic decision-making game plan for all your branding initiatives? Most advertising managers have a media plan a page or two long that an agency has produced, showing how their advertising dollars will be spent. The game plan I am referring to is the overall philosophy and management tool that keeps every aspect of branding on track.

The game plan acts as a compendium of sorts—a concise yet comprehensive strategy of how branding is executed in the marketplace. It covers all touch points of the brand and the rules for their implementation. Rather than leave this to chance, your game plan should include a branding decision tree that allows the manager to ensure that every branding decision is accretive to the overall brand experience.

The game plan is a document created to communicate the advertising and media plan. It serves as a guide for the organization's internal teams, including the company managers and franchisees, and provides crystal-clear direction to the agency. The compendium provides further explanation of how the advertising plan was created and how it will be managed. These strategic decisions should be reviewed on an annual basis to ensure that the entire branding program is in unison.

Below are the key elements to include in your branding game plan:

Market research and demographics

Utilizing market research, the targeted audience of your brand communications should be based on demographics, program selection, and scheduling guidelines. Demographics should cut across the following attributes, and all brand activities should be vetted against these targets:

- Age range
- Male/female ratio
- Total annual income
- Employment ratio
- Marital status
- Ethnicity

Program selection refers to the review of a program's content to ensure that it's consistent with the advertiser's desired brand image and its demographics. Scheduling guidelines assist in steering programming placement and frequency and delivery of media.

Flights, weights, and spots

Next, determine the game plan for when and how to communicate your brand. Flighting refers to scheduling periods of activity and inactivity on a TV and/or radio schedule. A period of activity is called a flight, and a period of inactivity is called a hiatus. Flighting is typically used to cover a long period of time, such as a year, within a limited advertising budget that does not allow advertising for fifty-two weeks. TV weight refers to the number of target rating points (TRPs) scheduled in a flight. TRPs are the standard unit of TV measure. Quantitatively, a TRP is equal to 1 percent of the target universe. Radio is a better medium than TV for building frequency. However, the fragmented nature of the radio market and the consumers' listening patterns limit the cumulative reach that radio can deliver. Unit length refers to the duration of a commercial spot/radio broadcast.

Day parts

Based on the demographics of the targeted audience, the brand manager needs to determine the optimal day parts for the messaging. Day parts deliver different audience compositions (e.g., daytime delivers a high percentage of women). There is also a correlation between a spot's audience and its relative cost. Prime time delivers a large, broad audience and is, therefore, the most expensive day part.

Electronic media

Now you need to execute the brand communication, and there are numerous options from which to choose. Television delivers the highest reach of any medium. The sight, sound, and motion of television allow the advertiser to communicate a message in a highly memorable way and to shape a visual into a recognizable image for their brands. Spot television offers the flexibility to target a specific local market in a programming environment consistent with the advertiser's brand image. Spot airtime for cable television is often much more expensive than broadcasting and does not have as large a reach. Cable television is limited because it only reaches paid subscribers. Spot radio is competitively purchased from local stations and can be easily targeted by market and demographics. Radio commercials are relatively inexpensive to produce, which enables brands to change messages more frequently. Since radio has no visual, it is less expensive than TV.

Nonelectronic media

There are other ways besides electronic media to deliver your brand message. Outdoor advertising (billboards) reaches a large percentage of the population, but because people on the go see it, billboard advertising is appropriate only for brief messages. It's best used to reinforce an established brand. Newspapers reach a wide cross section of the public, which makes it hard to target a specific audience. Other options include solo direct mail and marriage mail.

Sponsorships and promotions

You can communicate your brand through sponsorships and promotions as well. For instance, the brand may be aptly communicated through the sponsorship of local sports teams. By sponsoring these teams, the brand is allocated spot time during broadcasts, as well as occasional mentions by the game announcers. In addition, the brand may receive signage in the arena and mentions in printed promotional materials. Lastly, aligning the brand with a corporate charity communicates that the brand is an upstanding corporate citizen. Sponsorships and philanthropic involvement help communicate the brand's community responsibility.

Social media and the web

An overall brand game plan would not be complete without addressing social media. Setting up a company Facebook page, LinkedIn profile, Twitter account, and YouTube channel—each vertically integrated into your overall brand communications—enhances your brand presence. These social media enable the brand to be nimble with its messaging and, if integrated into an overall brand strategy, provide cost-effective touch points for key followers.

Your brand communications should work in unison regardless of the medium used. Each variable within these media—from program selection to day part mix—should be determined within a cohesive strategic branding compendium. Not only will the efficiency of your strategy be intact, but it will also yield greater results.

Creating an Advertising Plan

As you have probably gathered by now, I am a firm believer in planning for success. Whether it is operational excellence or outlining your procedures and policies, prudent planning creates stronger execution and efficiency. While planning may come second nature to me, I am surprised at how many operators leave their success to chance.

I have the opportunity to speak to a number of audiences on advertising and marketing, and one of the questions I ask is whether or not the audience members have created an annual advertising/marketing plan. Invariably, the operators who have an annual plan are in the minority. It is odd that most operators are fairly regimented in their routines until it comes to investing in advertising.

My guess is that most operators are intimidated by advertising to a certain extent and thus avoid the process of planning their investments. While it is true that there are some buzzwords in advertising, it is nothing more than having a cohesive communication plan for your trade area. With that in mind, here are some key items to include when developing an annual plan:

Outline goals
What do you want to accomplish? This may seem like an elementary question, but your goals will determine what type of ad plan you create and follow. If your goal is to increase new customer traffic, then a plan that addresses marketing activities throughout your three-mile trade area is critical. If, on the other hand, your goal is to sell more to existing customers, implementing loyalty programs and combo deals, for instance, are both designed to raise your average ticket. Throughout the year, you may find that you weave in both of these strategies.

Determine budget
Once your goals are determined, it is time to earmark investment dollars for your plan. The budget will help determine how meaty your ad plan will be throughout the year. Most operators determine their ad investment dollars as a percentage of their sales. That way, as sales grow, more

money is reinvested in the business. While this may alter some of your plans as sales projections fluctuate, it is much easier to adjust from an annual foundation than to rely on month-to-month planning.

Set to a timeline

This leaves the creation of an ad plan that can be executed throughout the year in a cohesive way. Most operators miss this part of the planning. Operators will say, "We have a plan," but a collection of one-month ads that fail to work together is not a cohesive long-term strategy. This approach lends itself to chasing the next shiny object.

Integrate the message vertically

Once the key dates are determined, identifying the vehicles to be used—i.e., electronic, print, social, POP, and so on—is next. Regardless of the sequence, it is imperative that each of the vehicles communicates a theme, which is commonly known as vertically integrating the message. Limited ad investment funds can stretch considerably further if each of the vehicles reinforces the message. If it is about the burger of the month, then all ads during that month should promote that burger.

Communicate to your team

Your staff is the critical link to a well-executed advertising plan. Failure to communicate when the vehicle will be reaching customers or the content of the message will blindside your staff when a customer reacts to an ad. There is nothing more frustrating to a customer who comes into a store then an ill-informed staff member. All the time spent planning and the investment to bring in that customer is for naught.

Post analysis

Lastly, in order to make your dollars work harder in the future, it is essential to judge and measure the success of the dollars that have already been spent. If something works—repeat it! If the investment underperformed, go to plan B and modify your annual plan. While your plan should create a cohesive strategic foundation, it is not etched in granite. It can be modified as vehicles are analyzed. Create a plan for success and fine-tune it throughout the year.

Local Store Marketing for Retailers

Local store marketing (LSM) should be a critical, constant component for driving retail sales. In many cases, it forms the building blocks for your customer point of differentiation, and your existing staff can execute many LSM tactics for very little money. Retailers should look at the following ideas to prop up their sales:

Improve visibility

Has your store become part of the landscape? Have you become retail wallpaper? Create excitement outside your four walls to draw attention to your store. A-frame boards at the street, cold-air balloons on your roof, mascots waving in crowds, searchlights, and so on all create and increase visibility.

Nudge your customers

Those retailers that have customer lists can reach out to their customers by e-mailing or calling, inviting them back to your store. All it takes is a friendly reminder to keep your store in customers' minds. A customer list is only powerful when it is utilized.

Create customer loyalty

Introduce a customer loyalty card and provide incentives for your core customers to visit your stores more frequently. Use these same loyalty incentives to turn casual customers into core customers.

Start product sampling

Want to entice trial of your core products? Deliver product samples to businesses in the three-mile radius around your store. Be sure to hand out flyers with your product samples, and then watch the sales roll in.

Create new customers

Establish new relationships with businesses in your three-mile radius by offering gift packages of your proprietary products. Contact local hotels and businesses to promote your products to hotel guests and business-people, and set up meetings with the local chamber of commerce and surrounding schools or churches to hype your store as a great venue for their next event.

Launch special recognition days

Everyone wants to be recognized, so create an event at your store that recognizes and appreciates certain groups of customers, such as specific businesses, age groups (e.g., kids' day), or students.

These are just a few proven LSM tactics a store can implement immediately for little or no cost. Local store marketing is critical to your overall strategy. The most successful retailers win the battle for customer traffic because they make an operational commitment to local store marketing. They know local store marketing captures the entire customer base in the critical three-mile radius around their store. In addition, they know that implementing local store marketing is low cost or no cost. Successful retailers infuse their promotional campaigns with local store marketing, building a strong foundation for sustained, long-term growth.

Marketing to Kids

Children have been marketed to for years. Retail industry titans have recognized that targeting children and winning their loyalty can carry on throughout their entire lifetimes. In some cases, this lifetime customer completes the cycle and introduces some of the same brands to his or her children. Establishing brands in the minds of our children can be powerful.

I remember joining the Pepsi-Tiger Fan Club as a kid. For about thirty dollars, I received outfield tickets to select Detroit Tigers games, Pepsi wristbands, a hot dog and a drink, and autographed pictures with the Pepsi logo, all packaged in a Pepsi mini duffel bag. My parents would load up the neighbor kids, and we would all go to the game. We were excited to be a part of this club, and consequently, it was no wonder that Pepsi was my beverage of choice growing up. Membership at such a young age carried great significance.

Kids want to feel significant in their own lives and in the lives of their parents. Joining the Pepsi-Tiger Fan Club meant a lot to me as a kid, in that it established a feeling of accomplishment and acceptance as a club member. I was proud to be associated with the Tigers, and Pepsi was the benefactor of my beverage preferences for many years. Developing marketing programs that make kids feel important has a tremendous influence on their buying patterns in the future.

Here are some considerations for marketing to kids:

Make it an adventure

Kids love intrigue and adventure. Creating a learning experience that also informs kids about your products is an excellent way to captivate their minds and capture their loyalty. One of my favorite adventures in kids' marketing was conducting store tours at Little Caesars. Kids were able to see how pizzas were made and in most cases, were allowed to make pizzas themselves and eat them afterward with their parents. Invariably, Little Caesars became the pizza of choice for the family, as fond memories of that excursion were recalled. A field trip to Little Caesars was always at the top of a kids' list of wants.

It's a digital world

It is a different world today than when I was a kid. According to the National Consumers League, "nearly six out of ten parents of so-called 'tweeners'—children aged 8 to 12—have purchased cell phones for their kids. Only 4 percent of those tweeners have basic phones with no Internet or texting access. About half have mobile phones with texting capabilities, another 20 percent have non-smartphones with texting and web access and 27 percent have smartphones."[1] That's a world that will continue to grow, and marketers need to be aware how to tap it. Creating an interactive link to your products rather than a passive advertisement will help cement the memory.

Step into their world

If you want to market to a kid, think like a kid. The character Josh Baskin in the movie *Big*, the twelve-year-old turned thirty, becomes effective at creating kids' toys because he is, in fact, still a kid. Watching the interactions of kids with other kids or with products offers a tremendous glimpse into how a kid thinks. I often sit back and marvel at how many clues kids give you just simply by observing them. A kid like the Josh Baskin character will not hold back in his or her assessment of a product or its attributes. A kid either likes it or doesn't and isn't necessarily politically correct in his or her opinion. Watch, listen, and learn.

Be a hero to their parents

Developing programs that benefit kids and parents is a win-win. When I was at Little Caesars and Clark Retail Enterprises, I developed coupon book programs in which kids sold coupon books on our behalf to raise funds for their teams. It was a simple-to-execute, effective program that benefited teams, parents, and my companies. The programs' goals included ease of execution, reduction of the company's cost of team sponsorship, building the brand in our community, and making money for the teams. They achieved all four, and parents were appreciative

---

1 National Consumers League

of the programs. In the end, the kids were happy and patronized our companies.

In reaching out to children, marketers often rely on the instant gratification offer of a prize or toy. While that may capture a child's eye once, it also commoditizes your product in their eyes. I would argue that attempting to reach a kid on a deeper level establishes a greater loyalty to your products and a life-long connection.

Creating a Corporate Communications Plan

Fire. Aim. Ready. If this is your communications plan, you may want to read on.

Amazingly, many companies do not think about communication—either internal or external—until it is a necessity. A crisis occurs, a reaction follows, and in many cases, the company does not necessarily put its best foot forward. A strategic communications plan should be a part of your overall business plan and can provide the clarity that is required in both good times and bad. Developing the process for communicating on an ongoing basis is critical in order to maintain a consistent message as well as a continuous forum from which to communicate.

Even companies with fewer than ten employees can have an effective communications strategy that enables them to articulate company news efficiently. In the case of my company, my website acts as the key repository for everything Gray Cat, and all news and information is disseminated to Twitter, LinkedIn, Facebook and YouTube. This helps organize information and create a cohesive communications strategy—even for a small company.

Once you have the basic distribution structure in place, developing the content is the next critical task. Rather than just develop news willy-nilly, ensure that a well-thought-through strategy is in place regarding content development. Timing and sequencing of topics are critical to having your audience stay with you. There will be ample opportunity to infuse new content as it is warranted—these items are just icing on the cake. Let's take a look at the core elements of a strategic communications plan:

Don't be afraid of the media

The first step is getting over being intimidated by the media. There should not be any fear in dealing with the media—they have a job to do and often are looking for news. Help them! Next, develop a list of all key media contacts and get their e-mail addresses. Be proactive with your contacts in order to create relationships in advance. In addition, target specific industries that would be beneficial for your business. Over time, your goal should be to enhance your company image through communications, as this helps soften distressing news and provides accessibility for interviews. Lastly, develop reasons for meeting the media and build those relationships.

Create news releases

Once you have established your media contact list, it's time to start to develop news content. Keep in mind that information may have to be tailored for each of your audiences, but the core message should stay the same. Determine what elements are critical, and conclude your news release with a consistent boilerplate that provides a quick paragraph on your company. Lastly, determine how the news release will be distributed and by whom.

Employees and stakeholders

Other audiences to include in your strategic communications are employees and stakeholders. Keeping your internal teams informed is vital. There is nothing worse than having misinformed employees and stakeholders attempting to communicate your vision.

Communicate to key vendors

Often overlooked is proactively communicating with your vendors. Many company owners feel compelled to keep vendors in the dark in order to keep them at arm's length. My philosophy is that vendors work better on your behalf if they understand how their role fits in your overall communication strategy. The more they are informed, the better decisions they can make to enhance their support of your brand.

Internet/Intranet media kit

In years past, having a hard-copy media kit—press releases, biographies of senior management, news items, and so on—was an excellent way of putting your company in a nice, neat package. Today, websites can act as the media kit and allow the flexibility to post updates on your company in real time. In addition, your website expands your reach far more effectively than hard-copy media kits. Save the dough and go electronic.

Media policy handbook

Lastly, if more than one person manages your communications or if you want to have greater structure within your organization, consider developing a media policy handbook. This guide can come in handy for developing consistency in dealing with the media, particularly if there is a crisis. Crisis management tests the mettle of any organization, and winging it only exacerbates the situation.

Creating and managing a strategic communications plan requires upfront work. Once it's in place, communicating a consistent message will not only be effortless, but highly productive. The media, employees, stakeholders, and vendors will all be singing from the same songbook, which ultimately translates into your customers being well informed about your company and brand.

Creating a Public Relations Plan

Public relations is a powerful tool in spreading the word about your store or business and its brand throughout the community that is often overlooked. Whether you are creating news, sponsoring an event, or contributing to a charitable organization, a prudent public relations strategy can create the following benefits:

- Provide low-cost brand awareness that's not perceived as advertising
- Help develop strong relationships with community and business leaders
- Provide another avenue to establish the credibility of your store and brand

Public relations can incorporate a number of items, and they should be interwoven in a consistent theme. At the beginning of the year, identify key people, events, and community tie-ins that you want to be a part of and create a cohesive strategy linking these activities. The obvious public relations tactics are the high-profile, low-cost events in order to gain exposure. More subtle tactics, such as networking, can contribute equally to improving your visibility. Some key ideas to include in your overall public relations strategy are outlined as follows:

Network with local leaders

Identify key leaders in your community and put forth a schedule to meet a minimum of two per month. Your list should include the chamber of commerce president, fire and police chiefs, youth organization leaders, strategic business leaders, and other key networkers. Associating yourself with these tippers will quickly and efficiently cascade your brand and its activities throughout your community. Consistently getting in front of these key leaders keeps you on the minds of your customers.

Create news

Working with the local newspapers to generate news regarding your store or brand is an excellent way to get a third-party endorsement. Many writers and editors are constantly looking for local flair from area businesses, and it's up to you to entice them. Feed them information on an ongoing basis, and they will appreciate your stream of idea starters. Tell them about new items or new employees, for instance, to fill the hopper.

Community events sponsorship

Building an important link to community events is another excellent opportunity to grow the business in conjunction with your marketing activities. Tying in with the school system on programs that reward students for outstanding achievement is a nice way to gain exposure, as are fundraisers, car washes, and contests. Chamber of commerce events provide the opportunity to get to know the other businesses in the area. Lastly, organizing store tours is a great way to get families to visit together.

Adopt a school

This is an excellent partner program that benefits both the local school system and the store or business. Working with the schools, you can customize a program that creates goodwill for your store and the school. This is a great way to win the hearts of kids and their parents as well. Help support a local school with monthly hour-long life sessions that tie to your store in a fun, memorable way.

Help a charity

Some of your local store marketing programs are designed to increase awareness of your brand; others you establish because it's the right thing to do. Working with charities enables you to give back to the communities in which you are located. Charitable work, when tied with vendor promotions, can be a great experience for your staff as well as a way to drive traffic to your store and benefit the charity.

Inform your vendors

Your public relations efforts should not be limited to your trade area, media, and your customers. Keeping your vendor partners informed on and included in your plans enables all parties that can influence your location to share a common vision. Include vendors on press releases; share strategic business visions; and ask them to support, as well as participate in, your success.

Ask your customers

Lastly, one way to tap into the minds of your customers is to ask them for feedback. More often than not, customers who are asked frequently about their experiences will share insights with you. In addition, formalizing a written survey or having customers give you their contact information enables you to target marketing efforts directly to them in the future. Rewarding customers for filling out satisfaction surveys can provide valuable information from your key sales source.

Public relations can be a great way to become known in your community and help foster relationships that your competition won't be able to touch. This ongoing community relationship building with both customers and suppliers can prove to be a vital part of your overall brand effectiveness. Savvy operators who master the art of relationship building may be able to spend less money on advertising to enhance their brands.

Forming an Advertising Co-op

When a multiunit organization begins to grow, one common step in the process is the creation of advertising and purchasing co-ops that enable stores to pool their financial and strategic resources. Generally, co-ops are determined using designated market areas (DMAs), of which there are approximately 210 throughout the United States. Every zip code belongs to a designated market area, and multiple counties make up the DMA. Forming a co-op allows all participating stores within that DMA to share the costs by combining funds to provide market continuity, delivering a single message to a large geographic area.

Creating and investing as a co-op brings all stores in a geographic area together to help deliver common brand benefits as well as increasing awareness. Over time, this can lead to greater market share for the brand. Combined with the obvious buying power that co-ops enjoy through lower cost-per-thousand investments, co-ops can position the stores to achieve greater sales.

The benefits of co-ops go even further and put systems in place to:

- Provide continuity and focus;
- Enhance cost efficiencies and strategic consistency;
- Create franchisee relationships beyond marketing;
- Allow franchisees to focus on operations; and
- Establish an approval process for franchisees through voting mechanisms.

Once you have decided to form a co-op, the details of how it will operate must follow. Here are a number of items to consider:

DMA definition
Nielsen television–based DMAs are determined by counties and follow the general guidelines that if more than 50 percent of the population in that county receives their television signal from one market, that county is in the majority-market DMA. Fringe counties often argue that they do not receive the same coverage as core counties, but nonetheless they still receive the majority.

Co-op scope and quorum
Once the co-op is formed, you'll need to establish guidelines in order to maintain its integrity and that of its members. Quorum guidelines are established in order to prevent a small group of members from getting together over coffee and determining how to spend co-op funds on behalf of the entire co-op. With a franchise organization, stores usually become eligible to vote on co-op issues only after they become operational, so they have some skin in the game. A minimum of 50 percent of

the stores and 50 percent of the members need to be present in order to form a quorum and allow a vote. In addition, members who are present may vote on behalf of another member by means of a proxy.

Co-op member contributions

Co-ops are designed to locally enhance any plans that may be in place at a national level. Co-op contributions and purchasing are accretive to those national plans and, when vertically integrated with the national message, can help deliver greater results. Most franchise organizations set two levels of contributions based on a percentage of sales: national ad fund contribution and local marketing co-op media fund. The national contribution levels are usually contractual; the franchise agreement may state the minimum level for co-ops.

Voting rights

Voting rights should be determined in advance of the formation of the co-op. Determine the best route for a democratic resolution. I have been a part of many co-ops and have seen a wild assortment of voting structures within them. The best one, which protects both the small and large franchise owner, is one store, one vote combined with a two-thirds majority of franchise owners. This ensures that a franchisee with multiple stores can't run amok within the co-op and protects those with the most at stake. Co-ops should be able to increase members' contributions through this voting method, and only franchisees that are current in their financial obligations to the co-op should be eligible to vote.

Co-op member protection

Determine if any additional provisions are needed to protect the members of the co-op. For instance, if a franchisee is selling his or her store, he or she should still be required to contribute up to the day of closing. In addition, since the franchisee is leaving the system but the store is not, credits for previous contributions should not be allowed. Once a contribution is made, it stays with the co-op. Lastly, all co-ops should establish how they plan to deal with franchisees that become delinquent in their contributions yet still gain the benefits of the advertising.

Forming a co-op is a significant event in a company's history—it states that the company has arrived. Co-ops assist in growing the brand exponentially, adding topspin to the overall brand message of the company. If administered properly, co-ops are a terrific way to increase customer recognition of the brand and foster an environment in which market share and sales increase significantly.

Help! I Have to Deliver a Presentation
What is it about public speaking that drives people nuts? Many studies have shown that, when asked what registers the greatest fear in humans, most people find untimely death less frightening than speaking in public!

- Public speaking or humiliation
- Peer rejection
- Untimely death

It is hard to believe presenting to groups causes such angst, but the benefits in free advertising are too good to pass up. As with many things in life, I believe it comes down to one thing and one thing only: preparation. Those who are thoroughly knowledgeable in their subject matter and their delivery find presenting not only easy, but also actually energizing.

One of the goals I have always had when delivering speeches is to know the material so well that I deliver the content in a nearly ad lib fashion. This casual delivery style keeps the audience engaged through both delivery of content and vocal inflection. In the early days of my speeches, I used to have three key words highlighted in my speaking notes for each slide. I would ad lib the slide, but I always made sure that I covered the three key words—that was the solution to delivering the message. Now, I practice speeches so much that the ad lib sections and anecdotes flow seamlessly to capture the essence of the presentation.

Rules of thumb

In a nutshell, make the presentation entertaining! Presentations should be inspirational; exciting; well thought through; and yes, entertaining. From the look and feel of the presentation to its delivery, it is critical to keep the audience dialed in. Specifically, I prefer the following as my simple rules of thumb:

- Black background with vibrant colors to pop off the slides
- Kabel Ultra Bold font for the best readability—not everyone is sitting in the front row
- No more than three bullets per slide—short and to the point
- Graphics on every slide—think entertainment and interest
- Presentation should be timed to about one minute per slide—keep the audience engaged

Storyboard it!

Before you start creating slides for your next presentation, plan what you're going to say. Storyboard the flow of the speech first; it will make your presentation more cohesive, and it will be easier to create the slides. Believe me, time spent up front in mapping the sequence will save you more time when you're creating the slides. This storyboard process will help you clarify what you want to say and when and how you want to say it. The flow of the presentation is equally as important as the content of the slides.

Never, ever read slides

Raise your hand if you have been in the audience when a presenter read the slides word for word—positively riveting! Don't be that guy. The audience can read the slides—keep them brief and to the point. Accentuate what's on the screen with anecdotal tidbits that enhance and personalize the slide. Keep the presentation moving so that the audience does not fall into a trance staring at a slide with one hundred words on it for five minutes.

Be a storyteller

Personalizing your speech is an excellent way to deliver a message. Anecdotal examples of real-life stories that help make your point create a longer-lasting impression on the audience. In addition, these interjections of personal experiences enable the speaker to humanize the points and allow the audience to create commonality with the speaker. The more the speaker can make the content his or her own, the better the reception from the audience.

Be prepared—practice!

Now is not the time to go lightly—this is the area that will make or break your speech. You *must* practice your speech to the point that it flows effortlessly from your mouth to the audience. In your mind, you need to know not only where you are in your presentation but also what is coming up next. I always love it when I get in the zone where I am simultaneously delivering the speech and thinking about what I am presenting next. Or as Wayne Gretzky, hockey Hall of Famer, would say, "Skate where the puck is going, not where it's been." That is being in the zone.

Overcoming the fear of public speaking is solved through one thing only—preparation. Know your stuff, be well rehearsed, and your delivery will be seamless and well received. The rubber-chicken circuit is not for the faint of heart, but with proper planning and preparation, you can unleash your inner orator.

GrayCat
Enterprises, Inc.

CHAPTER 6

FACILITIES, REAL ESTATE, AND CAPITAL MANAGEMENT

Prudent Facility Management

It was the situation that everyone dreads. Out of the blue, the anxiety-inducing request was made—the CEO had summoned me to his office. Thoughts raced through my head—mostly bad thoughts, mind you—of why I was being asked to join him and the COO in an impromptu meeting. Had I messed up a marketing budget? Did I misspeak at a press event? Did we miss gross profit projections? This cannot be good.

"We wish to have a word with you," it started out. As my career flashed before my eyes while the CEO went on and on, I started to build my case in my head. Then I noticed that his tone was actually complimentary, and he was saying that my departments were excelling. Then it dawned on me—I was being set up for more work! "We have decided that we want you to add another department to your group. We want you to head up facilities."

Upon hearing that, I mustered up my most eloquent response and asked, "What the [heck] do I know about facilities management?" To which they responded, "You are a smart guy; you will figure it out." In five short minutes, I had assumed all facilities management for fourteen hundred stores in addition to my other departments. I walked back to my office and started to figure it out, and they were right. I did. It dawned on me in time that facilities management was nothing more than managing projects and process. Once I got past the shock, I realized that this was right in my wheelhouse, and this is how the facilities department was comprised.

Repair and maintenance (R&M)

Anyone who has ever owned and operated a store knows that stuff breaks. Equipment, building structures, and any moving parts all fall victim to wear and tear. Setting aside a budget that addresses items as they break as well as preventive maintenance programs creates a proactive approach to managing your store. The customer expects a well-run and well-operated store that projects an updated, clean look. An ongoing R&M budget and plan keeps your store investment well tuned. Most of the expenses in this category are considered stay-in-business investments—they need to be made in order to keep the facility up and running.

Capital management

This is the most intriguing part of facility management. Capital management involves facility investments that are more discretionary in nature—in other words; these investments are expected to return incremental revenue and profits to the store. New store builds, adding new equipment, expanding existing footprints, and so on all constitute discretionary investments. A good rule of thumb for the expectations for the profits generated from these types of investments is around 20 to 25 percent. That means that the aggregate investments will pay for themselves in four to five years.

Construction

Construction is generally included in the capital management section, but by breaking it out, you can associate all the activities of building a new store. Designs, permitting, planning, build out, and post analysis can all be tracked on a per-project basis. In addition, assigning capital labor expenses to engineers allows for the project to capture all associated expenses for a more representative ROI analysis.

Environmental

In our case, not only did we have fourteen hundred stores to manage, but also eight hundred of them sold gasoline. Of course, any time there is a gasoline spill of fifty gallons or more, it becomes an environmental issue that has to be reported to the state, and plans to remediate the situation are put in place. These plans involve outside contractors, state officials, and internal personnel all working in concert to clean up the mess. In some cases, this can take years to complete, so managing the processes of each spill is specific to the issue and the state in which the work is to be completed. Let's just say that it is an extremely complicated process, so it's best to avoid any spills!

Purchasing

It is astonishing to me how much money can be saved through a prudent purchasing process. From paper clips to phone plans to shipping, the number of dollars that are lost due to not reviewing expenses on a line-by-line basis are staggering. One example I remember saved us nearly $200,000 annually for fourteen hundred stores, just by rightsizing our waste containers for size and frequency of pickup. The stores didn't see one hindrance to their ability to operate with this rightsizing initiative, and $200,000 fell to the bottom line. Other savings came from consolidating phone plans, renegotiating shipping methods, and so on. The money is there to be saved, if the process for saving it is implemented.

Overall management

Lastly, for companies that do not feel that they have adequate in-house resources to manage facilities, the option of outsourcing the management comes into play. In this case, the facility manager is the key puppet master for a team of subcontractors who manage the daily requirements of the facilities. Generally, a monthly management fee is agreed to, based on the amount of work expected. This type of management enables the company to remain focused on its core business while still maintaining its stores.

While I was in shock leaving the CEO's office that day, in hindsight, it was a terrific learning opportunity for me. The processes and procedures required to manage one thousand-plus stores can create value for for the enterprise if done properly. Without that oversight, dollars are lost and forgotten.

Maintaining a Facilities Database

There comes a time in every multiunit retailer's business cycle that he or she wants to launch a new product that requires a reconfiguration to the store. I am not talking about a raze-and-rebuild, but rather something as simple as sending a new piece of equipment to the store that houses the new product. That sounds straightforward enough, correct?

The challenges arise when the equipment gets to the store, and the manager asks, "Where does this go?" and proceeds to find a home for it. Over time, with each new product launch, more and more stuff gets sent to the store, and before you know it, each store is configured vastly differently. With every new launch, rollouts become increasingly problematic and a burden for the facility.

It is critical for the multiunit operator to get his or her arms around facilities management in an organized fashion. Maintaining a central repository of every store allows key decisions to be made with all components of the store considered. Does the store have space? Is there enough electrical? How will this affect the current floor plan? With a centralized store database, each of these questions can be vetted in advance of a rollout.

At a minimum, here is what is recommended in a centralized, store-by-store database:

Overall facility

Capturing the exact dimensions of the site including the floor plan is essential. All too often, strategic discussions regarding multiunit rollouts hinge on the fact that the stores involved will be able to accommodate the initiative. A detailed site plan of the location—both interior and exterior—provides answers to a number of questions when it comes to the viability of the rollout at the store level. Gathering this information in advance makes the process of planning strategic initiatives immensely more efficient.

Equipment

Next in the database is a detailed list of all the equipment that is housed at each of the stores. The equipment location within the store should be identified in the floor plan; this list pertains to the make and model of the equipment. For most retailers, growth in store count occurs over time and equipment used in the stores does as well. It is critical to know what version of the equipment is currently in place. As long as you are at it, you might as well check the size of the electrical panel. Failure to have an accurate listing of the equipment on hand will result in a number of headaches on rollout.

Financial history

The store-by-store database also provides the opportunity to link store-specific financial information for all locations. The database will enable the users to know the historical sales, margin, and expenses for any location. Combined with the physical store attributes, the financial components of the store help guide decisions on future investments for this particular location. While one would like to have a one-size-fits-all rollout, prudent management should view capital expenditures with a more discerning eye.

Capital investments

Previous capital investments should also be tracked on a store-by-store basis. Is this a store that has responded favorably to previous upgrades? Or have repeated investments failed to deliver the expected returns? Managing your capital investments on a store-specific basis helps increase the aggregate ROI for the entire portfolio. For those retail industries that are faced with environmental issues, namely the gasoline industry, tracking the historical environmental activity at the store level is critical.

Store characteristics

Over the course of developing your database, you may find that certain stores dovetail from an attribute standpoint. These attributes may be physical (large versus small stores), demographic (urban versus suburban versus rural), or even age (new versus old). How you classify your stores is entirely up to your organization, but in doing so, you may be able to cluster like investments based on these characteristics. In addition, if the assigned characteristics provide a glimpse into the predictability of future investments, then your dollars will go that much further.

Pictures

Lastly, what store database would be complete without a pictures library of each location? As the adage goes, a picture tells a thousand words, and having a pictorial database on each store is essential. That being said, random pictures of the store will not cut it. A sequence of pictures should be taken at each store the same way—that way, comparisons are easily made. How you develop the sequence is up to you, but consistency is the key. In my days of taking pictures, I started with the exterior from preset locations (e.g., the southeast corner of the lot) then moved on to the interior. I would capture the interior floor plan in the same fashion overall, then by merchandising section.

Creating a store-by-store database may appear to be daunting at the beginning, but the benefits of having that information available at a moment's notice are invaluable. Strategic and tactical decisions on key initiatives are much more easily made and executed. While the task of starting is daunting, the execution can be divvied up among members of your team who are in the field. Come up with a step-by-step plan and begin to build your database over time.

Managing a Retail Real-Estate Portfolio

For the multiunit operator, managing a retail real estate portfolio is tricky business. Keeping winning stores in tip-top condition—both physically and financially—is the key to long-term success. The best multiunit operators prune their portfolios in a proactive way over time, minimizing the risk of the organization being saddled with underperforming legacy stores that become dead weight for the company.

Understanding which units are continually contributing accretive EBITDA to the group of stores is critical for maintaining the health of the enterprise. Not only do the high-performing stores contribute to today's bottom line, but they also add substantial value at the time the chain is sold.

While some real estate portfolios consist of owned properties (with or without a mortgage), others are made up of leased properties or a combination of the two. In either scenario, the manager should be working in concert with operations to determine which properties should be divested and which properties should be kept and improved, perhaps through capital investment. Here are some key areas that should be front and center for the real estate manager:

Know lease term dates

Just knowing the term dates is not enough. A prudent manager needs to know all the key trigger dates that lead up to the term date. Working from those milestone dates, the manager should set up a game plan to evaluate the long-term viability of the property—especially leased property. Hanging on to dead-weight properties is the ruin of any multiunit operator.

Stay on top of exercise dates

Missing an exercise lease date may obligate the chain to another three to five years at an undesirable location or even worse, cause it to inadvertently lose a high-performing store. As with the term dates, there are many steps leading up to the decision date, including a thorough vetting by the operations team of the long-term viability of the unit. Real estate should lead this exercise in order to keep the organization on track with the key deadlines and time the process so that a discussion can take place with senior management prior to the exercise date.

Manage remaining options

As with everything, negotiations should take place when key critical deadlines are near. When a potential change may be enacted—either artificially or by a hard deadline—levering that time period to negotiate remaining options is optimal. If the store is an underperformer, simply do not exercise the next option. On the other hand, if the store is a long-term strategic "must have," then asking for additional options buys the company peace of mind.

Renegotiate rents

In addition to managing options, it never hurts to present a market as-sessment to the landlord to renegotiate the rent, using the trigger date of the option as the call-to-action catalyst. Everything is up for negotia-tion, provided that you have done your homework and can make a com-pelling case. In today's up-and-down economy, a lot may have changed since the company exercised its last option some three to five years be-fore. The squeaky wheel gets the oil, and being proactive with your ne-gotiations will produce a more viable portfolio.

Divest and relocate

Sometimes, the best option for a site is to sell or relocate the store. If the site is fee simple based (owned), selling the store is an option, and allocating the capital proceeds into strengthening the existing portfolio makes sense. With a leased site, letting the option expire and redirecting the customer database to a nearby store can solve two problems for the company—stop the bleeding at the underperforming store and move a suspect store over the break-even threshold into profitability.

Managing a retail real estate portfolio takes a lot of forethought and coordination with the operations staff, but by instituting an ongoing pruning strategy, the organization can continue to prosper. Falling in love with legacy stores despite their underperformance is to the detriment to the chain. In the end, letting go may be the best strategy to improve the viability of the chain.

Capital Management Process

Hopefully your business is growing and cash flow is strong. If that is the case, what a fantastic scenario to be enjoying! Now, you have to determine the best ways to put those earnings to use. The live-for-the-moment entrepreneur could simply enjoy his or her profits and pull money out of the company for his or her own personal fun. For those owners who carry debt on their businesses, paying down debt with the incremental cash may be an option. Lastly, reinvesting in the business is a third alternative, improving the strength of the company.

The reinvestment of capital is among the most proactive ways to grow your business. Inherent in the decision to reinvest should be a capital management process that directs the flow of capital not only to enhance returns, but also to minimize budget mismanagement caused by capital creep.

Developing a series of procedures ensures not only that projects stay on budget, but also that the best returning investments are prioritized. It is easy to fall victim to investing capital only in the sexy projects—e.g., new store builds, and so on—but a solid capital management process should eliminate the bias of projects and solely invest in the best returning ones. By utilizing the following guidelines, your capital management process can become more streamlined as well as positioning the company for greater financial growth.

Capital process

Clearly articulating the process of capital management to your team is the best way to inspire fantastic ideas from the field. The front liners are interacting with your core customers on a daily basis and probably have the best sense of what investments could be made to improve that experience. Therefore, educating your field staff on not only the process but also the benefits of identifying opportunities for investment engages your team while enhancing productivity. Bubbling up ideas is only one step in the process but a crucial one. Conveying that the owners of the company welcome new ideas and are willing to invest in some of them sends a powerful message to the team.

Capital request form (CRF)

It may seem mundane to have projects submitted with capital request forms, but this is the first step in determining whether the project is a "need to have" or a "want to have." Identifying projects with business plans and expected financial targets inserts a layer of discipline into the process of capital investment. All too often, ideas for investment fail to reach their targeted goals because the owner of the idea has not thought through the details of the request. This discipline of understanding both the soft and hard costs of the project combined with the expected margin uplift from the investment is the only prudent way to ensure success.

One-store investment model

In order to project the potential upside of a capital investment, build a financial model to track the investment against the return. Most financial models include areas such as existing financials for comparison, net present value of money, payback time periods, internal rates of return (IRR), cost of capital, EBITDA projections, and so on. Your CPA or business analyst should be able to create a pro forma that will enable you to add in the specific metrics for each project. This discipline of benchmarking the project before a dollar is spent provides the necessary advance filter when estimating the return of the proposed project.

Capital projections

For larger organizations, creating a summary table for all concurrent projects not only keeps these projects on task, but also helps manage the overall cash flow of the business. The capital projections summary should be a spreadsheet that tracks all capital investments by month, quarter and/or period. Generally, maintenance capital—the investment cost of staying in business—doesn't expect a return on the dollars spent. Therefore, the summary should be broken into two types of capital— maintenance and discretionary—in order to carve out the discretionary expenditures for ROI purposes.

Cap labor worksheet

Lastly, capitalizing some of the labor involved in capital projects helps capture the fully loaded cost of the project. Much like hiring a general contractor to build a house and including the cost into the overall bud- get, allocating a percentage of your facility personnel in the form of cap labor helps capture the entire investment. In some larger organizations, facility personnel may be fully capitalized over a number of projects without the cost of their salary and benefits hitting the G&A expense line. Said another way, if there were no capital investments, the facility person might no longer be needed at the company.

Capital investing can provide tremendous upside to the business and keep the company growing for years to come. Prudent business own- ers who have worked extremely hard to generate revenues and profits should not give it away through shoddy capital management. Rather, instilling discipline into their capital procedures can attain continual growth.

Making Prudent Capital Investments

Unlike operational expenses that are used to run the daily business or working capital to purchase inventory, money invested in the business that yields incremental income is known as capital investment. Generally, these investments are made with a long-term expectation in mind, and the return is achieved through added earnings.

Business owners are faced with many capital options over the life of their operation, and depending on the state of business, all are viable. The best operators are always looking to grow through ongoing investment by plowing a portion of their earnings back into the business. They identify the best income-generating projects, bring them forward with detail, compare them with other projects and prioritize them to identify the projects with the greatest merit. Detailed projects with solid business plans would then go to a review committee to determine the best investments and timing. This discipline and forward-thinking mind-set enable operators to stay ahead of their competition and position their businesses to maximize opportunities.

In general, determining which projects to pursue should follow a process along these lines:

- What we want to do and why
- Cost and return on investment
- Competitor information
- Store management information
- Trade market information
- Punch line: Why should we make this investment?

With that in mind, here are some key items to include in your capital investment management program:

Form a capital review committee
Even if it is only you and one other person, setting up a capital review committee creates discipline in determining the most efficient way to invest dollars back into your business. Bouncing ideas off one another and comparing potential investments make the process more scientific and less anecdotal. The committee should get together monthly or quarterly to review projects for consideration, check on the status

of projects already in the queue, and conduct post audits on projects that have been previously approved and implemented. The goal of the committee is to improve the business through sound management of investments.

Stay-in-business capital

Stay-in-business capital is exactly what it sounds like. It is required capital to keep the business in operation. Known as maintenance capital, these investments keep your operation in shape by fixing broken equipment or renewing software licenses for example. While this is a necessary part of keeping your business viable, there are few expectations for incremental revenues from these expenditures. That being said, combining these capital expenditures with revenue-producing discretionary projects should produce an aggregate return on investment.

Discretionary capital

Discretionary capital investments, on the other hand, are designed to generate incremental revenue over a period of years. Generally speaking, capital targets are in the four- to five-year range for payback on the investment. Discretionary projects take the form of system and infrastructure improvements, quick-payback projects that are accretive to earnings in the short-term, and long-term strategic investments. At its simplest method, combined with stay-in-business capital investments, store operators should reach a targeted payback percentage covering four to five years. More complex methods of capital budgeting are internal rate of return or discounted cash flow, which take into account the net present value of the cost of money.

Identify compelling projects

One of the most pertinent issues of which to be cognizant is that a capital budget is not an allowance—returns are expected. As importantly, returns are expected above and beyond normal operating returns. In other words, if anticipated revenues are to increase 5 percent without capital investment, you must add the return from the capital investment to your already anticipated increase. If your project is anticipated to have a five-year payback, then it is imperative that the earnings from that project are carried forward for each of the five years. Targeting the projects that are proven winners shows discipline.

Team role in capital management

Everyone on your team should have an active role in your capital management process. In many cases, the best ideas are those that bubble up from the field. Lean on your team to identify and develop a business case for each investment. This will engage your team and, as importantly, empower team members to deliver results on the investment. Your staff will be well positioned to deliver on the business plan if they are involved in the entire process.

Capital management can be the lifeblood of your business and, if properly executed, provide the means to long-term growth. The discipline surrounding the selection of where to invest your hard-earned dollars is critical in order to prudently pursue the best returning projects as opposed to the most popular ones.

Project Management

The nice thing about not planning is that failure comes as a complete surprise rather than being preceded by a period of worry and depression.

—Unknown

If you get in a car in Chicago with the intention of driving to Los Angeles, the GPS rarely plots the California portion of the trip while you are in your driveway. Rather, the GPS methodically and sequentially plots each road to take in order to reach the desired location. Project management follows the same logic: a series of key tasks or steps that have to be completed in a systematic process in order to meet the desired outcome. The trip to Los Angeles from Chicago can only happen if the tasks of traveling through the Midwest and the Rockies are completed first.

This type of thinking seems elusive when it comes to business project management. Ask someone to map out the many steps required for achieving the desired result of managing a project, and many times you get resistance, suggestions of overkill, or simply a deer-in-the-headlights look. Yet the dollars at stake as well as the operational disruption to the organization seem secondary to the tedious task of mapping the process in advance. No one would jump in a car and start driving without a map nor should they start a project without a plan.

Lacking a plan almost assuredly locks in failure as much as putting the wrong project manager in place does. There is a specific skill set that is required for project managers that enables them to manage to an on-time, on-budget conclusion. It is critical for the organization to identify those key people to lead projects or, as an alternative, outsource to industry experts.

The key components of project management are highlighted next:

On time, on budget
This should be the mantra of every project manager. There should be nothing more fundamental in the mind of the project manager than completing the project on time and on budget. All too often, project managers view their projects in a vacuum, but rarely are tasks within an organization mutually exclusive. Failing to comply with an on-time, on-budget philosophy not only causes the project at hand to fail, but also risks the failure of other, related projects.

Know the endgame
Determine in advance what a successful project conclusion looks like. The most successful projects have a clear vision in mind from the onset.

Poorly managed projects fall victim to duplicative resource allocation and cost overruns known as capital creep. Capital creep can be crippling to an organization, since it not only sucks away future dollars to be invested back into the company, but also layers on added expense that diminishes the overall return of the project.

Resource management

Let the fighting begin! Project management is all about organizing systems and sequencing processes in order to efficiently complete the task at hand. Implicit in that mind-set is identifying the resources that are necessary to knock out the work. The challenge is that resources are finite, and competent people are always in demand. There can be some intense competition for solid resources—over allocation of their time is an ongoing concern.

Practice "war-gaming"

Imagine if you could anticipate issues in advance—that is what war-gaming is. Play out possible scenarios, and anticipate broken pipes in advance of their actually breaking. Scheduling a resource for a task only to find out that he or she is going on vacation is an avoidable broken pipe. By laying out as many steps as possible against a time line, a project manager should be able to recognize obvious hiccups in the process in advance and devise possible solutions.

Be realistic

Rome was not built in a day, and your project will not be either. Setting realistic goals not only for the project but also for the approving committee is paramount to managing expectations. The project cannot be built for free nor can it be completed in an afternoon. Realistic goals and timetables need to be continually communicated and are crucial to the overall perception of the project.

Daily business impact

An organization's challenge in managing new projects is that there is still a day-to-day business to run. Rarely does a company have an idle body that can manage a project exclusively. Smart organizations are the ones that identify this in advance and either outsource the management of the project or adjust internal teams to minimize disruptions to daily operations. Organizations that fail to recognize this impact will not only see their project fall short of expectations, but also run the risk of their daily operations slipping.

Deliver the goods

At the end of the day, the project manager has a fairly clear-cut task at hand: deliver a completed project on time and on budget. Managing the project can be fraught with missed tasks and time challenges, but the successful project manager will attempt to minimize them. Leaving the entire project to chance will guarantee only one thing—a failed project.

Integrating Acquisitions

You can grow your enterprise organically, building your overall portfolio of stores through the development of ground-up store build-outs; you can acquire other locations; or you can do both.

While organic growth is slower overall, the process allows the enterprise to manage the pace and design of the stores in order to provide consistency throughout the chain. Growth through acquisition can quicken the pace of expansion but cause havoc with consistency, since you are buying other people's vision, and managing the integration of the acquisition becomes an art in itself.

Acquisition integration takes place on many fronts, including brand management, cultural integration, system dovetailing, and process management. Since a number of economics depend on the integration of the acquisition, on boarding must be extremely detailed to capture and accentuate the synergy of the deal. Failure to integrate properly will result in missed opportunity and a diminished return on capital employed.

Here are some key areas to consider with the on boarding of an acquisition:

Over communicate

There is nothing worse than an integration process that fails to communicate the overall objective and detailed action items to both the existing and on boarding teams. Creating a detailed, step-by-step project plan that is communicated to all parties in advance is absolutely critical to keeping the project on plan and the angst at a minimum. Every area of the project should be detailed, including culture, brand, systems, inventory, and auditing in order to successfully manage the integration project to an on-time, on-budget conclusion.

Cultural migration

Acquisitions can be emotional for all parties involved. The employees of the acquiring company will be saddled with incremental work to make the integration smooth. Employees of the acquired company will be concerned about the security of their jobs. It is vital to ensure that everyone is crystal clear on the expectations their roles within the organization. In addition, migrating the acquired company into the culture of the existing enterprise should be gradual rather than abrupt.

Brand management

Obviously, the most apparent part of the acquisition involves the de-branding of the acquired location and the transition to the new brand. While this may be the end of an era for the original brand, the newly branded location can often lead to a rejuvenation of sales—especially if the brand is now part of a progressively expanding portfolio of stores.

The newly branded store may be able to capture increased market share simply because of their association with a growing brand.

Systems integration

Price-book management, back-office integration, inventory procedures, and the flow of sales data all have to be managed throughout the transition. It is critical that all stores continue to operate while the transition is in place. Every procedure must be vetted in order to ensure that data can be rolled up appropriately to the corporation. If a glitch happens here, the ongoing benefit of growing through acquisition will be compromised.

Manage the physical stuff

Equipment, store fixtures, exterior signage, and all moving parts need to be accounted for in order to ensure that the acquisition is whole. Full inventories of each store—both equipment and product—need to be complete as of the day of transfer. The acquisition of multiple locations requires a fully trained team to hit the ground running. The economics of the deal depend on the appropriate transfer of all inventories.

Track the synergy

Lastly, understanding the economic synergy of the deal in advance will highlight the need to track the ROI to hit that goal. All too often, companies that grow nonorganically tend to move on to the next deal before the existing deal is complete. This growth pattern can spell doom for the acquiring company in the long run because opportunities for enhanced ROI will be missed along the way. Providing a post audit on each deal is one way to hold the enterprise accountable for the capital investments.

The growth of an organization is vital, not to mention invigorating for the entire team. With corporate growth, opportunities for personal growth abound throughout the organization. As I have been a part of both types of growth models in my career, I can personally attest to the vigor each strategy provides. There is nothing more satisfying than successfully integrating a group of stores into a portfolio and adding accretive value to the organization. Done well, the company prospers. Fail to plan for the on boarding of an acquisition and the results will not only harm the stores coming on board, but also weaken the acquiring company.

Relocating a Store

The lease is up at your existing location, and the new center down the street is happening. The thought of relocating your business is daunting. When will you find the time? Will you lose customers? An important decision faces your brand: Do you relocate your business?

Thousands of retailers face this dilemma every year and while staying put may be the correct decision, in many cases, relocating your business can provide an updated look for your store and jumpstart a business that may have plateaued. Serious risk is involved in relocating, but if managed correctly, tremendous upside is attainable.

Relocating your existing store is a two-step process: building a new store while simultaneously de-branding the existing location. Carefully consider the timing of both projects. Neither closing the existing store prematurely nor maintaining two locations is optimal. For the customers, a seamless transition is the key to maintaining their allegiance.

Note: Store de-branding is not an effortless process, and upward of forty to sixty man-hours may be required to complete it, depending on store design and format. The goal is to return both the interior and exterior of the existing store to their original state.

Make it positive

It is all in the positioning of the message. A store relocation should be celebrated as a positive event—one that has only been enabled by the patronage of the customers. Position the relocation not as an inconvenience of moving, but rather as a reward of a fresh, new location for the customer base. It is through your customers' ongoing support that the relocation has been made possible. Highlight the incremental features of the new location in addition to any new store designs or merchandise that will be added. New features and merchandise will reinvigorate your customer base.

Tap existing customers

Think about how much you have invested in your customers. Relocating your store should not and cannot cause you to lose any of your customer base. Your goal should be not only to maintain your customer base through local store marketing, but also to grow it by moving to a better location. That is the reason you're relocating in the first place, yes? So each and every customer needs to be addressed so there is no margin for error or miscommunication. The cost of retaining your existing customers is far less than the cost of acquiring new ones.

Overcommunicate

Just when you think you have communicated enough, double it. It is better to be safe than sorry, and while you are fully aware that your store is relocating, your customers have interests outside what is going on with your store. While planning your relocation, start proactive messaging at least two months in advance, with flyers going out to every customer. Include the reason for the relocation, the key dates, and an appreciation for their business. For instance, if your business is phone based (call-in orders) and your phone number is going to change, send every customer home with a refrigerator magnet with your new number on it.

A picture is worth a thousand words

Many people are directionally challenged, so adding a map of both the existing location and the new store to all communications is critical. A large sign in the window helps existing customers envision where the new location is. It is also critical to place signage at the new store during the build-out. That way, if a customer wants to find the new location in advance, signs will assist in their navigation as well as providing information to new customers.

Create incentives

While all the communication in the world may still not get your existing customers to the new location, incentives may be the next option. Much like a grand opening, your relocation needs to be promoted with both existing and new customers in order to make the transition as seamless as possible. Providing incentives to your customers as you would with a grand opening is a terrific way to get them to seek out the new location. Once they have made the effort to find your new location, your ongoing marketing communication should keep them coming back to the fresh new environment.

Celebrate a grand reopening

Yes, you do have something to celebrate. Your business has thrived enough to enable an investment in a new location. Do not be afraid to tell the world about your ongoing success. A relocation gives you an excellent opportunity to shout "I am alive and well" and position the relocated store as a thanks to existing customers who will now be rewarded with a fresher store. Once the relocation is complete, plan a grand reopening, communicating the activities to the new and previous trade areas.

Planning your relocation is as critical as the planning you did when you opened your store. Many years of customer cultivation cannot be risked by a poorly executed relocation. Manage your timeline, overcommunicate to your customer base, and make sure that you treat the opening of the relocated store as a grand opening. Proper execution will ensure that your existing and new customers will jump-start your new location with an influx of sales.

Managing Technology throughout the Company

I am putting myself to the fullest possible use, which is all
I think that any conscious entity can ever hope to do.

—The HAL 9000
2001: A Space Odyssey

When it comes to technology for your business, it is easy to get carried away with the latest-and-greatest gadgets and solutions. Everyone wants to have the newest shiny thing. In larger organizations, managing technology can become burdensome because of competing and duplicative technology requests. Left unfettered, the company technology platform can resemble a spaghetti bowl over time. Often new technology requests are submitted without any business case to support the investment.

I am a big proponent of having nontechnology business leaders play an active role in determining an organization's technology solutions. While it is critical to include an IT perspective for technical interface, having non-IT personnel drive technology solutions often leads to decisions based on the business needs of the organization. Any technology request then requires a business plan to support the investment.

Form a technology committee

This is the start of your technology-approval process. Create a technology committee with personnel from cross-functional departments. Consider selecting operations, marketing, accounting, technology, and finance members for this team. This committee will create the process for submitting technology solution requests to the organization, as well as prioritizing and ultimately approving the requests.

Develop a submission process

Inherent in a well-thought-through technology strategy is developing a process for submitting ideas. Following the garbage-in, garbage-out mind-set, developing a detailed process for submission will help weed out the "nice to haves" and focus the committee on real, tangible solutions. This process should include both the technology solution identified and, as importantly, the business case that justifies it. For approved projects, a monthly communication should be sent to the organization recapping the activity of the committee.

Focus your projects

A technology committee creates focus throughout the organization. While it would be great to have every new version of technology that gets released, that is impractical and costly. The committee can help with providing a high-level perspective on the entire enterprise, since it is considering all requests. All too often, departmental requests are created in a silo, with only the impact on that department considered.

Need to have versus nice to have

This is a biggie. It is easy to feel that one iPhone becomes obsolete as soon as the next iPhone is released, but when the committee runs the technology requests, the nice to haves usually fail for lack of a business case. The committee allows the organization to run with an unbiased interference with respect to technology. The committee is charged with improving ROI on technology solutions, and since it is cross-departmental, there should be no pet projects.

One project, big picture

I have headed a technology committee in the past, and the greatest aha moment for me concerned the number of similar technology solutions that were being presented from different departments. Had all these requests been accepted, the organization would have overspent IT dollars and created duplicative solutions to the same issues. The committee allows for its members to rise above the fray and view the technology requests within the big picture. The committee's goal is to ensure that any approved request is accretive to the entire company.

Create a business case

This is the best way to clear out the clutter. Ask employees what they need from a technology solution, and the committee will be inundated with ideas. Ask them to submit in a business case (cost justification for the investment) along with their solution, and the number of ideas is significantly reduced. The business case for a technology solution not only helps in identifying whether the investment is worth it, but also forces the author to think about how this solution interfaces with the existing platform.

Post analysis

Lastly, carefully measuring the business case pro forma against the actual cost/return of the projects holds both the submitter and the committee responsible. The goal of the post analysis isn't to call people out, but rather to provide an unbiased financial review of the project. Without this type of post analysis measurement to hold the team accountable, the committee will serve no purpose.

GrayCat
Enterprises, Inc.

CHAPTER 7

FINANCIAL MANAGEMENT

Organizational Transformation—A Step Forward

In business, it is essential to know the path just traveled. Most organizations take a look back at the preceding one to two months to evaluate their financial results and attempt to make rhyme or reason of them. They hold lengthy discussions to either justify or explain the results—which there is no way of amending. In my twenty-plus years of experience in corporate America, I found that the majority of the time is spent reviewing past performance.

Taking a look back is critical, but where I believe most organizations miss opportunity is failing to spend more time looking forward to events and initiatives that they can truly influence. Learning from past events and results, organizations should adapt their upcoming initiatives to address or even enhance past performance. This is where a company can truly inspire fantastic results.

With an introduction of KPIs into their management practices, organizations can begin to transform into forward-thinking action companies. My rule of thumb is that organizations should look back one month and look forward three months. With every passing month, this sequence of review stays the same, reforecasting three months in advance. This process enables a prudent organization to focus its energy on future business, rather than wallowing in past performance. The numbers are what the numbers are, and they warrant review, but they will never change.

Know the results

If you are sitting in a meeting discussing the financials of the company from one or two months ago and the results are news to you, there is a problem. Systems and procedures are lacking at an organization if the results are communicated at the end of a month without any prior discussion of trends or KPIs. Processes need to be interjected along the way so that critical decisions can be made throughout the month, and the review of the previous month is cursory at best. Leaving your team in the dark until the month-end meeting creates dependency, as opposed to sharp management.

Reforecast on the fly

With your annual plan in hand, now is the time to learn from the first month's results and reforecast the next three months from both a financial and an initiative standpoint. Prior to the start of the annual plan, projections were based on expectations of the business. Now with a month in the books, shortfalls should be addressed with new initiatives. This strategy keeps the business approach fresh and, much like a coach making adjustments to the game plan at halftime allows for reactions to the real business environment. At the end of subsequent months, the process repeats.

Inspire solutions

Armed with data from the previous month and an enlightened team, collaborating on solutions for the upcoming three months should foster inspired targeted results. Create a culture that holds teammates accountable for past results yet lifts their spirits with group participation in solutions. If the group can craft answers to previous issues, each team member has skin in the game to ensure that the future goals are met.

Successful implementation and accountability breed more and more solutions. It becomes an inspirational culture.

Plan for success

As your team progresses throughout the year, more results should help crystalize the initiatives that are working and eliminate those that are not. By midyear, this transformation of forward thinking should point the organization to greater and greater success on each and every new initiative. Process and content will be further refined, and the success rate on deliverables should consistently improve. Over time, your team will know the score and hold one another accountable for delivering results in their respective areas of expertise.

Do it all over again

This isn't a one-and-done endeavor; this is an ongoing process. The discipline of reviewing one month back and three months forward creates a forward-thinking culture at your organization. Over time, the organization will see results in real time with an eye toward improving upon those results, not simply explaining them. The path of least resistance is waiting for results and attempting to explain them. An organizational transformation to a forward-thinking mind-set may unleash the true value of the enterprise.

Developing Your Financial Acumen

The art of understanding your business from a financial perspective is critical for any entrepreneur. Knowing your business will provide you the avenue for achieving both your short- and long-term goals. Today's cash flows are met, and solid financial acumen positions tomorrow's potential exit more effectively. While we would all like to be at the top of our game on day one, it is crucial to walk before you run when whipping your company into shape.

The key is to know your numbers. Knowing your numbers will make decision making easier. Developing key financial reports that offer insights into your P&L, capital ROI, cash flows, and the like will make you a stronger operator today and position your company for achieving maximum value in the future.

You should always keep the endgame—creating value in your enterprise for the potential of its eventual sale—on target in order to dovetail all your decisions. For any owner, the litmus test for each operational decision should be how it improves the overall value of the business. Short-term gains that add future long-term value are the ultimate goal. Throughout the process, you will hone your financial acumen.

Strategic financial planning benefits
Short-term financial business planning provides precise clarification of your vision both to employees and, indirectly, to customers as well. In addition, it provides a mechanism to gauge results by establishing a foundation for future growth plans, ultimately leading to a stronger long-term company valuation. In some cases, the strategy may be to exit the business—the ultimate payoff for the business owner—by maximizing the value of the company and telling the story of opportunity to potential buyers.

Create a financial accountability system
Begin with your prior year baseline and enhance it with accretive product development and improved sales and margin targets. Develop and manage new initiatives to achieve both incremental and capital-induced sales. Instill a process management system that rolls up financial activity to be reviewed monthly and reforecast quarterly. This ongoing monitoring of your financial results will identify items that are working in advance, as well as initiatives that are falling short of plan. For initiatives that fall short of expectations, generate new ideas to get your financial plan on track.

Quarterly forecasting

Breaking the plan into chunks enables you to better manage your plan, essentially becoming a rolling quarterly forecast financial model. Whether your tasks are for revenue enhancement or expense control, managing by quarter and segmenting tactical initiatives allows your financial plan to stay on course. It is no different than balancing your checkbook monthly—if you don't create the discipline to review financials in a preset time period, the year will end and goals will not be met.

Company valuation

Company valuation assesses the economic worth of an organization and, in a situation in which a company is going to be sold, what the price of the sale will be. If the company is public, a rule-of-thumb estimate is based on the stock price. The number of outstanding shares times the value of the shares provides the market capitalization of the organization. While this doesn't necessarily translate perfectly into the value of the company—many other influences factor in—it can provide a reasonable estimate. In private companies, the estimated company value is a little more difficult to calculate because not all factors are publicly disclosed.

Be accountable

Ultimately, it is all about accountability and understanding your numbers. You need to walk the walk by establishing prudent practices and routines that arrive at a common theme: knowing your numbers. Your financial accountability metrics should include, but not be limited to, the following:

- Creating balance sheets for the organization
- Calculating income and cash flow statements
- Knowing your income, expense, and monthly run rates
- Staying in tune with average sales and margin trends

The endgame

In order to maximize the value of your company, planning is everything. Equally important is understanding the elements of your business that can increase its value. Your company finances cannot be built on a house of cards, and when you create an offering memorandum to present your company to potential investors, it has to be built on ratable facts. Anecdotal explanations will be vetted thoroughly throughout a due diligence process and ultimately will be cast aside as just that—anecdotal. An offering memorandum presents the historical financial performance of the enterprise in the context of the marketplace and projects believable future expectations. A successful presentation is verifiable through due diligence and is not built on speculation and baseless projections.

In summary, your financial acumen business planning doesn't only provide the road map to where you are headed, but also identifies roadblocks to overcome in advance. It provides a common vision supported by tactical initiatives; each designed to create greater value in the enterprise. In the end, a business operator should know his or her vision and financial targets and how to achieve them. Without that map in place, the organization will not only flounder today, but also fail to capitalize on its potential tomorrow.

Tear Down the Expense Wall!

Every small business owner faces the same issue—managing his or her expenses. While most small businesses keep a keen eye on growing the top line—revenues—many fail to address their expense line items on an ongoing basis. Granted, when the business started, all line item expenses were carefully reviewed. But now that your company is established, when was the last time you went line by line on your P&L to see if you could pare expenses?

All too often, business owners become complacent with their run rates on expenses. For instance, it is a lot of work to change banks in order to reduce fees. But there are some real hidden savings in everyone's P&Ls that could move additional dollars to the bottom line. I think we can all agree, as business owners, that we would rather have the dollars ourselves than to blindly pay them to an Internet or phone company.

Establish a habit of reviewing each line item on your P&L a minimum of once annually. I use the trigger points for filing my taxes as my reminder that it is time to tear my P&L apart. Even if I can only shave a couple of hundred bucks off my expense line monthly, this exercise forces me to review my business on an ongoing basis. While a hundred-dollar savings may not seem like much (or maybe it does!), it all adds up and keeps the money where it should—in your pocket!

Here are some of the key expense line items that I make sure I review every year:

Health insurance

This one is a complete no-brainer. The changes that have taken place over the last few years with the passing of the Affordable Health Care Act as well as the changes that are forthcoming mandate that you look at and shop your health care every year. You will end up paying through the nose without ongoing monitoring of costs. What lies in store over the next few years with regard to health-care costs is anyone's guess, but don't be surprised if your costs accelerate significantly. Failing to monitor health-care costs on a frequent basis (perhaps twice a year) could end up eroding all your profits from the business. The dollars here can be significant, numbering in the hundreds or thousands per month.

Telephone expense

The telephone industry is an extremely competitive one, and plans are continually being modified. While most cell phone companies require two-year commitments, plans can change significantly over the course of those two years, and you should be prepared to switch based on your actual usage of your plan. If you have a lot of rollover minutes, it is time to reduce your allocation plan, thus lowering your costs. Find the plan that fits your actual use, and you may be able to knock twenty to fifty dollars a month off your expense line without sacrificing service.

Internet/cable/data expense

Cable companies and Internet providers are notorious for offering teaser deals to get you to commit to their services. Generally, these last from six months to a year and, if left unchecked, can significantly increase your expense line at the end of the promotional time period. Many business owners load up on all the extras during these promo periods yet never actually use all that they have committed to. This is a good time to pare down the services and only pay for the ones that you need.

Professional services

Most small businesses have to tap outside professional services throughout the year. These can range from attorneys to CPAs to bookkeepers and so on. Regularly monitoring the professional fees line can help shave dollars off your expenses. You may have needed some of these services early on, but perhaps there are some that you can minimize or even put out to bid. While most outside professional resources are selected on both price and trust, it never hurts to keep these resources honest from a pricing perspective.

Utilities

Much like with your phone and Internet bills, some common-sense cost savings in utility expenses can be easily implemented. Knocking a few degrees off your heat, adding light sensors that turn the lights off in unused offices, and following other general cost-savings techniques help shave unnecessary expense. While this is an area in which it is hard to gain any negotiated cost savings, getting by with less usage can save a dollar or two.

Rent/leases

One of the smartest decisions I made when I started my business was to minimize the need to rent an office. For service-providing companies, carving out a dedicated space within your house can save a significant amount of cash each month. You have to be disciplined to work from your house, but if you can pull it off, the break-even of your business can plummet. For those businesses that occupy commercial space, opening up a dialogue on rent reduction with your landlord and equipment provider is a way of letting them know you are on top of it and are shopping.

Travel and entertainment

Lastly, managing a widely variable expense line item like T&E can pay off handsomely. Technology continues to advance, and the pipe dream of videoconferences has now become a reality. While I can appreciate the need for face time with a client or customer, you may be able to augment your meetings with video conferencing via Skype or another platform. You may be able to shave 10 to 20 percent off your travel budget without sacrificing the benefits of in-person meetings.

The bottom line is that you should protect your hard-earned dollars by reducing expenses. You are in business to earn money for one person—you! Your hard work should be your reward, not the reward of a service provider or vendor. Build this expense monitoring discipline into your business annually, and you will ensure that the dollars that are earmarked for your business stay with you.

Strategic Market Analysis

Recently, I sat through a meeting with one of my clients in which we discussed the infamous question "Who are we?" that faces every retailer. As retailers grow—both in store count and in product diversity—the ongoing challenge is to keep a laser focus on what the brand really stands for. Growth for the sake of growth can deteriorate the essence of the brand faster than any other catalyst.

Developing a strategic market analysis is critical for companies that grow organically or through acquisition. For organically grown companies, the question is easier to implement with varying geographic nuances. Speed to market share is much slower with companies that build new stores (organic growth) than it is for companies that acquire locations. As I mentioned before, the challenge with growth through acquisition is that the company is buying someone else's dream. Folding that dream into the go-forward direction of the acquiring company is the toughest part.

Companies in growth modes are faced with the ongoing dilemma of keeping their expanding portfolios on plan with regard to their strategic branding direction. In concert with a store database, a strategic market analysis acts as a guidepost for every new store entity that comes on board. While the vision of the founders may be more aspirational, how an organization plans to grow often determines what their strategic market analysis ultimately identifies.

What do you want to be?

This is easier said than done. First and foremost, it has to be believable. Many brands aspire to be something they are not. If Waste Management were to claim they are the Tiffany of waste hauling, it would be a far-fetched stretch. Secondly, it has to be practical. I once worked for an organization that did not like a certain word that was embedded in the logo of the brand. Simple enough—we would remove the word. Until we learned that the estimated cost was north of $7 million, since the logo was on the stores, uniforms, packaging, letterhead, and so on. It was a great thought but an impractical reality.

Identify the roadblocks

As mentioned above, some roadblocks are due to the type of growth the company expects or the capital expense to turn a vision into reality. With an acquisition growth model, the strategic market analysis should determine on a store-by-store basis, a roll up of what could be, and that will determine who the company can be based on that model. When you buy others' visions, there are limits on how far you can influence your brand, unless you are simply buying dirt and plan to raze and rebuild at an inflated capital expense.

Fantasy versus realism

We all want to be best in class, but sometimes the reality is that we can't. Either through physical limitations or financial ones, the fact is that with a growth-oriented company, many outside factors influence who we can be. If money is no object, then the issue is solved. For the other 99.9 percent, prudent investment is clearly the mandate in order to achieve the ROI. It is time to check the ego, or your pocketbook will run amok.

War-game the reality

Start with a list of existing stores. How similar are they? What enhancements would be required in order to get them all to the same level from a strategic market branding perspective? Is it even feasible, or has growth over the years limited your ability to invest that much capital in your existing (and future) sites to align the vision? Going through this store-by-store will help identify the commonalities as well as creating a targeted strategic direction. Better to know this in advance than self-actualize, at a huge expense, halfway through your business plan.

Operationalizing your vision

Once a store-by-store list is completed, setting out a plan for capital investment is next on the list. This project plan must not only work for existing stores, but should also apply to new stores as they come into the fold. Store-count growth can be a wonderful thing, but left unmanaged when it comes to on boarding new locations it will quickly deteriorate the essence of your brand. Capital investments should be made to ensure that the strategic alignment of the stores is consistent and fiscally practical.

Four-Wall Analysis

When it comes to managing a profitable operation, knowing the key financial drivers of your store is paramount. Developing a four-wall analysis is helpful in better understanding both revenue projections and variable and fixed expenses. Few operators take the time to create a simple pro forma analysis so that they can clearly see what contributes to or detracts from store profitability.

Rather, they leave the P&L to their accountants on a monthly basis instead of managing to profitability on a daily basis. A four-wall analysis provides a simple yet effective way of managing the moving financial parts. Each retail store will have its own set of key revenue and expense line items. Managing to your store P&L will create greater overall profits than simply reading the results at month end.

Sample Four Wall Analysis For Foodservice Operation					Comments
Annual Sales	$300,000	$400,000	$500,000	$600,000	
Monthly Sales	$25,000	$33,333	$41,667	$50,000	
COGS					
Food (34%)	$8,500	$11,333	$14,167	$17,000	Sample food cost target for menu
Paper/Chemicals (3%)	$750	$1,000	$1,250	$1,500	Sample paper cost
Labor Range (18% - 10%)	$4,500	$5,000	$5,000	$5,000	Sample labor reduces from 18% at 300K to 10% of sales at 600K
Total COGS	$13,750	$17,333	$20,417	$23,500	Total food, paper, labor range - 47% to 55%
Gross Profit	$11,250	$16,000	$21,250	$26,500	
Expenses					
Rent	$3,000	$3,000	$3,000	$3,000	Sample rent for stores
Utilities	$700	$700	$700	$700	Sample utilities stay flat at any volume - no incremental
Communications	$200	$200	$200	$200	Sample flat usage rates
Insurance	$200	$200	$200	$200	Sample flat usage rates
Office Supplies	$150	$175	$200	$200	Sample nominal requirements
Printing	$200	$250	$300	$300	Sample nominal requirements
Repairs/Maintenance	$160	$180	$200	$200	Sample nominal requirements
Licenses/Fees	$40	$40	$40	$40	Sample flat usage rates
CC Processing	$400	$600	$800	$1,000	Sample credit card
Miscellaneous	$25	$25	$25	$25	Sample miscellaneous
Royalties (6%)	$1,500	$2,000	$2,500	$3,000	Sample Franchisee Royalty Fee
National Ad Fund	$250	$333	$417	$500	Sample 1% national ad fund.
Co-op Ad Fund	$500	$667	$833	$1,000	Sample 2% local co-op ad fund
Total Expenses	$7,325	$8,370	$9,415	$10,365	
Net Monthly Profit	$3,925	$7,630	$11,835	$16,135	
Net Annual Profit	$47,100	$91,560	$142,020	$193,620	

115

The benefits of creating the four-wall analysis are tremendous for the following reasons:

Sets goal-setting target scenarios

This analysis provides an assortment of the "what if" scenarios that an operator should be cognizant of in order to manage profitability. Most operators will have a ballpark idea of their P&L but will have no sense how a sales increase of 30 percent or a significant sales decrease affects their bottom line. By looking at a variety of revenue scenarios and their corresponding expense loads, an operator is better armed to manage his or her store.

Know the key drivers

Much like the federal government budget that largely consists of three key expense line items—Social Security, Medicare, and Medicaid—most operational P&Ls have core drivers to their budgets that, if left mismanaged, will crater their profits. In the food-service industry, for instance, those three drivers are food, paper, and labor. Fail to manage those three, and the remaining expenses are immaterial. Identify the key drivers in your operation, and manage these with a fine-tooth comb.

Understanding variable versus fixed expenses

Under different revenue scenarios, expenses will either be fixed (e.g., rent) or variable based on the volume of the store (e.g., utilities increasing with added hours/equipment). Lowering your fixed expenses to their lowest level through negotiation and managing the growth of the variable expenses are critical to improving profitability. The goal is to improve the delta between additional revenues and manageable expenses.

Overcoming barriers to growth

It seems obvious, but everyone wants to grow revenues. Well, almost everyone. Sometimes employees will resist growth because they aren't motivated by incentives and they don't have the desire to work harder servicing more customers. The pro forma scenarios should identify ways to reduce barriers to growth, not layer on more barriers. War-gaming different scenarios will provide the operator with ways to motivate his or her staff to embrace growth, not resist it.

Manage line by line

Sharp operators understand that the key to profits is in the details. Each line item should be scrubbed to provide the most efficient cost structure. One of my favorites is trash removal. This expense item is determined by the size of the container and the frequency of the pickup. If you want to reduce your expense for this line item, train your employees to break down every box, can, and so on and reduce either the size of the container or the frequency of pickup. Managing by line item squeezes dollars from your overall expense load.

Teambuilding buy-in

Lastly, make your P&L management a team effort. Share with your employees and educate them on the items that drive the profitability of the operation. If employees are unaware of how their contribution affects the P&L, then they are oblivious to managing profits and have no incentive as well. Getting your team on the same page is a critical step in running a tight, profitable operation.

In summary, knowledge is powerful. The four-wall analysis is a critical tool for any operator to embrace because it identifies *in advance* the key drivers of the operation and allows the operator to manage to stronger profits. Being proactive and taking ownership of each line item with a process and strategy to maximize profit should be the ongoing incentive for every operator.

Break-Even Analysis

One of the questions I hear most from store owners is "What sales volume does my store need in order to make money?" While it would be convenient to rattle off a figure off the top of my head, it undoubtedly is a store-specific number. What the owner is genuinely asking for is a break-even analysis for his or her store.

Earlier, I explained the importance of a four-wall analysis, creating a simple yet important profit and loss report on the store. Store operators usually understand the expenses associated with the daily operation of their store, but after layering on debt service, the break-even sales figure increases dramatically. Much like a homeowner with a mortgage and car payment, store operators who add large debt loads to their store's P&L find tremendous pressure to increase top-line sales. This added expense load is the difference between making it and folding up shop.

A break-even analysis takes it a step further to include the following:

- Variable cost percentage
- Fixed costs
- Debt service

ANNUAL BREAK-EVEN WORKSHEET

Step 1: Calculate Variable Cost %		STEP 2: Calculate Fixed Cost $	
COGS	25.00%	Telephone Expense	$1,500.00
Direct Labor (Management & Team Wages)	22.00%	Utilities	$2,400.00
Indirect Labor (Payroll Taxes)	8.00%	Rent, including CAM	$15,000.00
Employee - Management Store Expenses	1.00%	Maintenance & Repair	$1,500.00
National Advertising Fund	4.00%	Insurance General	$2,000.00
Local Advertising Co-op	1.00%	Taxes & Licenses	$1,500.00
Complimentary/Other	0.50%	Cash (Over) or Short	$1,500.00
Promo Items	1.00%	Bank Charges	$1,000.00
Discounts and Coupons	0.25%	Office Supplies	$1,000.00
Bad Debt (Bad Check)	0.50%	Operating Services	$1,000.00
Gift Cards	1.00%	Operating Supplies	$2,000.00
Credit Card Expense	2.50%	Pest Control	$1,000.00
Product Shrink	1.50%	Professional Services	$1,200.00
Royalty Fees	8.00%	Trash Removal	$1,500.00
	0.00%	Security	$500.00
	0.00%	Uniform Expense	$1,000.00
	0.00%	Employee Benefits - Manager/Team Bonus	$20,000.00
	0.00%	Debt Service: Principal Payments (Cash Flow Item)	$10,000.00
	0.00%	Debt Service: Interest Expense	$25,000.00
	0.00%	Other Expense	$500.00
Total Variable Cost %	75.25%	Total Fixed Cost $	$91,100.00

STEP 3: Calculate Contribution Margin %		STEP 4: Calculate Annual Break-Even Sales $	
One Hundred Percent	100.00%	Total Fixed Cost $ for 52 week period	$91,100.00
- (less) Total Variable Cost %	75.25%	+ (divide) by Contribution Margin	24.75%
= (equals) Contribution Margin %	24.75%	= (equals) Annual Break-Even Sales	$368,080.81

Here are four key items to consider:

Itemize variable costs

Add in all variable expenses as a percentage of sales. Obviously, this cannot exceed 100 percent, and the difference between 100 percent and the total of all the variable costs is your store contribution margin. Said another way, if store sales volume is $500,000 with an operating margin of 30 percent, the contribution margin would be $150,000.

Determine fixed costs

Calculated how much will be spent per category annually. Include all debt service charged to your operation. Want to lower your break even?

Think twice about leasing a new car for a company vehicle. These added costs burden the store P&L and in some cases put an unnecessary strain on the store's overall success ratio.

Create "what-if?" scenarios

While some variable costs are predetermined (e.g., royalty for a franchise operation), some may be managed through efficient operations. Both fixed costs and debt service may be managed lower as well. The best operators develop multiple break-even versions that span from best to worst case scenarios.

Reforecast quarterly

As a good rule of thumb, reforecasting your break-even analysis every quarter helps shine a light on your wins and challenges. This reforecast allows for the development of strategies and tactics for your operations team to address the shortfalls. This management is essential for maintaining successful store operations. To that end, develop tactics to address these shortfalls in both cost control and management as well as through revenue-generating initiatives in local marketing.

All too often, store operators have a sales volume in mind to be profitable but fail to recognize all the expenses associated with their businesses. The four-wall analysis (store P&L) combined with the break-even analysis is a way of helping store operators understand the importance of minimizing debt or unnecessary expense. In many cases, the stores perform well in comparison to their operation but simply cannot compensate for the added debt burden.

In the end, the piper always gets paid.

GrayCat
Enterprises, Inc.

CHAPTER 8

SUMMARY

Creating an Offering Memorandum

There comes a time in every entrepreneur's life when he or she wishes to leave the business. At that time, one of the essential documents for a business owner to create is an offering memorandum. An offering memorandum should represent the guiding path for the enterprise, mixing in a historical prospective and its relationship to its future expectations. All too often, business owners fail to reflect on the past as a learning component of where their businesses are headed.

Most business owners are good at developing tactical initiatives but have challenges in seeing how they connect to the overall financial performance of the company. The offering memorandum helps communicate not only the vision of the business for today, but also where it's headed. Articulating realistic expectations for the company enables prospective buyers to effectively determine whether to invest in or purchase your company. On the flip side, misrepresenting its value is an absolute no-no.

I am a solid believer in writing an offering memorandum that, if it fell out of your back pocket and someone stranger picked it up off the ground, would allow the reader to fully understand what your company has done and is expected to do. That is my litmus test for a solid memorandum. While an offering memorandum can encompass many components, here are the three essential areas to be vetted and addressed:

Business description

Each of these areas helps to explain the who, what, why, where, and how of the business. While the terms may seem elementary, remember that employees and/or investors need to understand the genesis of your company in order to embrace the aspirations for its future growth.

- **History:** Outline the driving force that prompted the start of your enterprise. In particular, communicate what marketplace need was addressed by its formation. This should also be reiterated in the five-year plan, especially if the initial needs have been modified.
- **Description of products**: Explain not only the company's products but also its share of revenue in the company business model. Include product gross profit and unit velocity on an annualized basis.
- **Company economics**: Explain how the company earns revenue from its product line against the associated expenses of the firm. Include all revenue sources from commissions to distribution to fees and so on.
- **Marketing strategies**: How does the company market its products? Explain the strategies that have been put in place that make the company's offering unique.
- **Marketplace opportunity**: How is the business positioned within the competitive landscape? What untapped opportunities will continue to grow the enterprise? Present the upside value of the business in a realistic manner to create interest.

Financial review

- **Historical financial and operating data**: The financial section of the offering memorandum is by far the most prominent section. Most transactions are made on a multiple of EBITDA, and that multiple can vary by industry and/or upside potential. Accurately accounting for the historical financial data helps place value on the company.

- **Description of assumptions**: Along with the actual financials, a section describing the assumptions that are being used in the projected five-year plan is next. These assumptions help explain and frame the discussion surrounding how the projections were put together.
- **Projected five-year plan**: The five-year projections take into account the historical run rates and the go-forward strategies of the company that enable it to achieve its pro forma. While the buyer and seller can debate this section, nonetheless it does attempt to tie the company initiatives to the corresponding financials.

Management

- **Organizational charts**: The organizational chart of the business should also be included so that the investing company can gain an understanding of the existing team. If the purchase of the company is part of a roll-up of companies, the acquiring party may deem many positions duplicative. If it is a stand-alone purchase, maintaining the integrity of the team is paramount for its continued operation.
- **Management biographies**: Lastly, the background of each of the key team members should be included in the package.

Communication is key when it comes time to exit your business. Being prepared and organized conveys a sense of stability and credibility for the potential investors. An accurate and powerful offering memorandum can be the difference between realizing your financial goals and not.

The Road Ahead

Launching and maintaining a small business operation is really hard. The amount of work that is required to not only survive but also thrive is monumental. But the rewards can be that much greater. You have sweated and worked your tail off, so why not put yourself in the best possible scenario in which to succeed?

Game-Changing Strategies for Retailers is designed to help coach, mentor, and pave a path to prosperity. While some small business owners will not be able to implement all the items listed in this book, working with and indoctrinating even a few of these suggestions will put you light-years ahead of other entrepreneurs. Yes, there is work to be done, but those who embrace the work up front generally reap the benefits of success in the end.

Having been a small business owner for more than a decade now, I am living proof that putting into place all the rigor and discipline that I have gathered from corporate America and applying it to a small business works. I have not only survived but have thrived, with both financial rewards and the freedom of time. While the former is certainly a blessing by earning money doing something I love, it's the latter—the freedom—that is by far the greatest reward.

71052364R00075

Made in the USA
Columbia, SC
19 May 2017